Hunting with Harris Hawks

bob dalton

Hunting with Harris Hawks
bob dalton

contents

Hunting with Harris Hawks is published by:
PW Publishing Ltd.,
Arrowsmith Court,
Station Approach,
Broadstone,
Dorset BH18 8PW
UK.

ISBN: 978-1-874110-40-8

First Hardback Edition
published August 2006.

Softback Edition published
April 2008.

© PW Publishing Ltd. 2008.

introduction

O ver the past few years there have been a great many books published on the sport of Falconry. Some of which have been by highly respected authors who have an undoubted knowledge of the sport and its day to day practice. Others seem to fall somewhat short of this ideal and leave the reader wondering just how much practical knowledge the book was based upon. Several of these published works have been either directly concerned with the Harris Hawk or have featured the species heavily. Therefore the question arises as to whether there is room, or even the need, for another publication on the subject.

Having taken the time and trouble to write just such a book then obviously I believe there is. This opinion is also based on the amount of phone calls, e-mails and letters I receive from falconers, both experienced and new to the sport, asking for help with certain problems. Most are simple to deal with and the solution would have been obvious with a little more experience. But I try and cast my mind back to when I first took up the sport and how a problem, that might seem insignificant to someone else, seemed a major one to me. I felt that a book with a bit of depth and a bit of substance, based on many years practical hawking in the field, might well stand up on its own merit and be worth the effort of writing.

Falconry is a sport that has been the ruling passion in my life for more than 35 years now. What started out as a hobby eventually became my full time living and I'm now in a position where I can indulge my love of the sport on more or less a daily basis. Back in the days when I had a conventional job I longed to be able to spend more time hawking. The winter season was always the time of my deepest frustration, when hawking possibilities were at their maximum and my hawking opportunities were at their minimum. Like everyone else around me I would go to work in the dark and return home in the dark five days a week. This left just the weekends free for following my passion. If the weather or indeed any other consideration meant that this all too short window of opportunity was taken away from me, then another restless week would be spent waiting for the following weekend to come around.

In an effort to spend more time hawking I took various jobs, some of which I hated, that involved working odd hours or even nights. I worked on American Air Force bases doing bird clearance work in an effort to be able to hawk more regularly. Although this gave me the opportunity to fly many more falcons and the occasional hawk, I wasn't actually hawking, merely exercising these superb creatures and probably calling on them to use less than half of their full potential. I even took a job in Austria which would supposedly give the opportunity to spend far more time actually hawking. I did earn a lot of money but didn't get to do any hawking of real significance. Accordingly I returned to Britain and followed what most would consider a more normal career path, doing my best to fit my falconry in with my work.

In the end, I decided the only way for me to be able to hawk as I wanted was to give up a very highly paid conventional job and work for myself doing what I wanted to do. I took the plunge some 20 years ago and have never looked back. Financially the first few years were not good but now things are as they should be and my hawking is probably as good as it can get. I hawk practically everyday of the season, here and abroad and enjoy tremendous sport both by myself and in the company of other falconers.

Practising the sport has taken me to many countries and introduced me to like minded people across the globe. A common interest seems to overcome language as well as cultural barriers. With modern methods of communication and travel the world is getting to be a smaller place and there really is no reason why falconers shouldn't think in international rather than national terms. For example, I always wanted to trap, train and fly a passage Harris Hawk at quarry in its truly natural environment. Then having enjoyed a few brief weeks of sport in its company, release it back to the wild. With a little help from friends in Mexico I achieved this goal. As I have with flying passage Peregrine Falcons at Ducks in the same country and Aplomado Falcons at Spur Winged Plovers in Brazil.

Attending field meets abroad is a good way to start for anyone wanting to expand their falconry horizons. Contacts are made and invitations to go hawking will inevitably follow. For those that have a consuming interest in the Harris Hawk then seeing them flown in different situations, climates and at different quarries should be of interest. As should be the opportunity of seeing them in the wild hunting both singly and in family groups.

In working on this book I am very conscious of the fact that what works well for one falconer does not necessarily work well for another. What I have put down is what has worked for me over the years and what hasn't. I have tried to be honest and point out mistakes I have made as well as the positive things. There will be those that offer criticism based on their own personal experiences and whose opinions differ to mine. Let me state categorically that I welcome such criticism and am just as open to new ideas now as when I first set out on my falconry career so many years ago. We should never stop being willing to learn and there is always a new wrinkle or way of doing things that can be of use. No one knows it all. Equally, there will be those that criticise out of ignorance, jealously or just plain bile. To those I can only suggest you get a life.

It is my hope that this book will be of interest to those that share my admiration for this unique species of hawk. If it helps someone who has a problem with their hawk or stimulates someone to try something different and get even more enjoyment out of their relationship with their Harris Hawk then the trouble of writing it will have been more than worthwhile.

My sincere hope is that this book proves to be of enjoyment to the reader and that long may we all enjoy practising the sport of falconry.

chapter one
the harris hawk

There can be absolutely no doubt whatsoever that the Harris Hawk, more than any other species, has totally changed the face of modern falconry and its practice. In less than 40 years it has gone from an absolutely unknown quantity to the most widely flown hawk amongst falconers throughout the entire world. It matters very little where you go in the modern world, with only one or two exceptions, the Harris Hawk will be there.

Often decried by many as being too easy to train and fly, it has often been compared rather unfavourably with other large hawks such as the Goshawk and the Red Tailed Hawk. This is undoubtedly a mistake. The Harris Hawk is unique amongst large hawks in that it is sociable and highly intelligent – therefore it needs to be approached and treated differently to other hawks that have enjoyed a longer association with falconers.

I know the following few lines will upset a lot of people but it is a fact of life that a Harris Hawk is easier to train than any other large hawk and the same is true of hunting with them. It has often been said that if it wasn't for the Harris Hawk then 90% of falconers would never have caught anything. A remark that I think is probably somewhat of an exaggeration but is nevertheless based in truth. Instead of maligning the species I think that these remarks tend to show that this particular species of hawk is highly intelligent and can make up for the shortcomings of those that sometimes choose to fly it. It is a hawk that is quick to learn and has a first class memory. Couple this to the fact that once manned it is generally very comfortable in the company of the falconer and it makes for an ideal hunting companion.

In fact, it is so intelligent that it can, if given too much free reign, end up hunting for itself and not for the falconer. I have seen so many Harris Hawks that have developed into complete self hunters that they are probably beyond the point of being brought back to what would truly be considered a falconer's hawk. Chasing a hawk through a wood as it pursues what it wants and only getting it back on the fist when it kills is not falconry. But hopefully how to avoid getting into this situation will be dealt with adequately later in the book.

The fact that Harris Hawks are both intelligent and gregarious can be traced back to the niche they fill in the wild and how they interact with each other to survive. The species is found throughout the Southern United States, Central America and South America as far down as Chile. As with all species of hawks the Harris tend to be larger in the northern part of their range and decrease in size as they reach the southern extremity of that range.

Juvenile male Harris Hawk.

The nominate species of Harris Hawk is *parabuteo unicinctus unicinctus* and there are two recognized sub species and these are as follows:

Parabuteo unicinctus harrisi.
These are found in southern Texas down through Mexico, with the exception of the north west region, through Central America to the Pacific slope of South America as far as western Ecuador and northern Peru.

Parabuteo unicinctus superior.
The range of this sub species extends from south eastern California, southwestern Arizona, south in western Mexico including Baja California, through to Nayarit. Much is written about the superior sub species of Harris, particularly by those that are selling captive bred youngsters, but they are in general only slightly larger and darker than the *harrisi*.

Parabuteo unicinctus unicinctus.
Almost all the rest of South America including Chile, Argentina, Paraguay, Venezuela and Brazil. Very similar in appearance to *harrisi* but flecked lightly with white underneath and also slightly smaller in stature.

In the field the Harris Hawk is very easy to spot with its long legs and tail and distinctive white upper tail coverts. Young Harris Hawks can quite easily be confused with other species but generally speaking they will be seen as part of a family group, which will contain adults and therefore make identification easier. Much has been made of and written about the fact that Harris Hawks will hunt in family groups. From my own observations in the wild this is true and I have seen quite large numbers of them hunting co-operatively. The largest number I have seen is 16 but more often the number is four or five. I have also seen many couples hunting together but have only ever seen an individual Harris Hawk on a couple of occasions. Normally, the fact that they are on their own indicates that all is not well with them and sooner or later they succumb to the attentions of other predators.

One thing that will strike the first time observer of wild Harris Hawks is their relative tameness and tolerance of approach by man. Providing no loud noises or sudden movements accompany your approach you will be surprised at just how close you can get to a pair or family group that are perched in Mesquite trees, Cactus or telegraph poles. These three items are the favoured look out spots of this species of hawk. From here they will look for a prey item and once spotted will attack in a pre-set and highly effective sequence. Males will go in at low level and try to flush and drive out the victim from any cover it has taken temporary refuge in. Meanwhile, the females will move into position and take stand from any handy vantage points ready to attack when the prey is flushed.

If the hunt is successful then there is a very definite and clearly defined pecking order when it comes to the hawks taking a meal. The alpha female will always eat first followed by the other females and then the males.

The other hunting method employed by wild Harris Hawks is prospect flying. This is where the group flies over a territory hoping their presence will flush a Rabbit, Jack Rabbit or Ground Squirrel. Small and medium sized birds are also taken as are lizards, rats and very occasionally carrion.

I have also watched a pair use ambush tactics to catch ducks in the central region of Mexico. Now, whether this technique is a general one or a specific action discovered by this pair I have no way of knowing. But as I have observered them use the technique many times over the course of three years it must be a deliberate ploy as opposed to an accidental series of coincidences. This pair hunts a relatively large man-made cattle drinking pond. It has a bank round three sides which is about two metres high and one metre across the top, small bushes and clumps of vegetation have gradually grown up on the sides and the top of the banks and offer quite good cover for a hawk. At first light the hawks make their way from where they have roosted for the night to the cover of one of the bushes on the bank overlooking the pond. Now it is a case of playing the waiting game.

Sooner or later some ducks will land on the pond and start to feed there. Once the ducks

Juvenile male and adult female on the fist showing the difference in both plumage and size.

are settled the male Harris Hawk will slip away from the pond using the bank to shield himself from the ducks. He will then fly low through the surrounding vegetation using the cactus and Mesquite to keep himself out of sight of the ducks. Once he is in a position that has the ducks directly between himself and his partner waiting in ambush he rushes in towards his intended meal. Needless to say, once the ducks realize they are under threat from the male they lift up and fly directly away from him. At this point they are still labouring to get up off of the water and over the bank and it is now that the female hurls herself out of cover and, more times than not, catches a duck. I have seen her take Teal, Mallard, Corn Ducks and even a female Pin Tailed Duck.

This really is a very clear example of not only the intelligence of the Harris Hawk but also its willingness and understanding of the need to co-operate when hunting. In normal circumstances only a really good slice of luck or a sheer fluke would enable a Harris Hawk to

Red Tailed Hawk. A species that was initially more popular with falconers than the Harris Hawk. But now has most definitely been surpassed by the Harris Hawk in terms of numbers flown.

The author with a freshly trapped adult male Harris Hawk in northern Mexico. This hawk was banded and then released.

catch a fully alert duck sitting out in a pond, but the collaboration means that the Hawks have a better than even chance of making a kill. I have twice seen the male make a kill when the duck the female was after had managed to evade her attentions and turn back, but the act of turning back has brought it straight into the talons of the opportunist male.

Breeding in the wild obviously takes place later in the northern part of the Harris Hawk range than the south. Mating starts to take place about three weeks before the first egg is laid and has even been observed taking place on the ground. But in a family group with more than one adult female, only the alpha female will actually produce eggs. The nest is an untidy affair made of sticks and twigs and lined with grass, leaves and green sprigs. Because of the lack of availability of tall trees, nest sites tend to be quite low and many are built on the top of Cactus. The only wild nests I have seen of any decent height were in Peru in a clump of old trees that were at least 20 to 25 metres high.

Between two and four eggs will make up a normal clutch and these are white in colour and sometimes adorned with a few light brown spots. The young develop quite rapidly and by 17 to 20 days are feeding themselves and spending a great deal of time involved in wing flapping exercises. The young will leave the confines of the nest altogether at the age of five to six weeks but will usually stay with the parents for another eight to nine months. In fact it is normally the onset of the following breeding season that is a contributing factor to the final dispersal of the youngsters.

I have been fortunate enough to have spent a lot of time assisting with the ringing of wild Harris Hawks and have therefore trapped a great many of them. The Bal-Chatri is the method I have always employed for trapping these intelligent hawks and it has never yet failed me.

Adult female Harris Hawk returning to the fist and showing why the species is also sometimes known as the Bay Winged Hawk.

The only problem is that the females are very wary and wait for the males to flush the prey. But as the prey is inside the trap it doesn't flush and the females look on as the males are being caught. Let me immediately point out that any form of trapping is illegal in Great Britain.

The only way round this was to put out several Bal-Chatri at any one time and to let each hawk come down to its own trap. The drawback with this is that it is essential to get the hawk out of the trap as quickly as possible so that it doesn't damage itself, but with this method we would often catch two or three hawks at the same time. The only thing to do was get them out straight away hood them up and put them in a sock and then ring them one by one and release them as we did so.

The bait for the Bal-Chatri would always be a dark coloured rat. I have tried white ones and also mice but was never successful with either. Because Harris Hawks can normally be approached to within 100 metres without too much difficulty then putting out the traps is very easy – even when operating on your own. It is merely a question of positioning the vehicle you are using between the hawk and yourself and then putting out the trap. When you then drive on after the briefest of stops the trap with its tempting bait will be in plain view.

If you are in a country such as Mexico and are trapping under license for falconry purposes as opposed to ringing, then selecting the hawk you want before putting your trap out is essential. You want to cause the minimum stress to any wild hawks and shouldn't trap indiscriminately. Careful study through binoculars will help you decide if the hawk spotted is the one you want or not. The only problem being that if it is a young female you are after (under no circumstances should adult hawks be taken) then you are probably going to have to trap several males first. After all, the males nearly always come to the trap first as a result of how a family group hunts. Young hawks will often join in the initial flushing attempts of the males and you may strike lucky.

Unless you live in The Americas then an aviary bred youngster is what the modern falconer is going to get the opportunity to fly, but don't let that be considered a negative thing. The reason the Harris Hawk has become the most commonly flown hawk in the world of falconry is that it is capable of taking such a wide variety of quarry in a range of differing

...ances and doing so in a reliable and enjoyable way. Trained properly it is a hawk that will constantly surprise you with its tenacity and ingenuity when it comes to catching prey. If care is taken over introduction they will happily work with dogs, ferrets and others of their kind. It really is the hawk for everyman. I stated in my introduction that I changed my life circumstances so that I can hunt my hawks and falcons everyday of the season and that I was dissatisfied with only being able to fly at weekends when daylight hours were short. But for many people this is their only option due to work, family commitments or a combination of both.

The Harris Hawk will still perform quite well whilst only getting limited exercise during the week and then being hunted at the weekends. It is not an ideal situation but more than any other species of hawk the Harris will normally still acquit itself well in the field. This has led to the species rather unkindly being referred to as the weekend hawk. This actually is far more applicable to those that fly it in this way than to the hawk itself. No hawk can possibly give its best if it is not truly fit and flown at quarry on a very regular basis. Most weekends, providing the weather is okay, does not really count as regular.

The fact that the Harris Hawk is highly adaptable and can nearly always be relied upon to give a good account of itself has helped to make it the popular hawk that it is today. Their appeal seems to be almost universal and I have seen them flown throughout Europe, in both South and North Africa as well as in North, South and Central America. Certainly in Europe they have replaced the more traditional Goshawk as the number one large hawk of choice. I can well remember attending an international falconry meet in Europe almost 20 years ago and there were four male Harris Hawks present and around 60 Goshawks. The same meeting two years ago saw that the balance had shifted very much towards the Harris Hawk, with them out-numbering Goshawks four to one.

The way the falconry world has embraced the species and the rate at which it has done so is quite astonishing. But I must say in all honesty that my own conversion was not a particularly quick one. Way back in the days when the species was still very new to our shores and hardly anybody had even heard of a Harris Hawk, let alone seen one flown, I was offered a freshly imported male. The hawk in question was some considerable distance from my house but I did make the effort to go and have a look at it. This was probably more out of curiousity than of any real deep interest in acquiring the hawk.

At that time importation of hawks was still very relaxed and relatively unrestricted, although getting decent hawks was still a problem. It was a case then that demand would always far outstrip supply. Passage and eyass Goshawks from Finland, Germany, Hungary and one or two other countries were still available occasionally in somewhat limited numbers. But generally speaking with a little patience the hawk you desired could normally be obtained.

When I saw my first ever Harris Hawk, sitting on its bow in the company of two others on a weathering lawn, my first impression was not one of staggering beauty and a burning desire to take it home with me. When I was told the price, approximately three times the current rate for a feather perfect passage female Goshawk from Finland, I instantly knew it would still be sitting on the lawn when I left. In fact it was to be many years later before I got my first Harris Hawk and this was almost a reluctant purchase. But it was one I have never regretted and has

Juvenile Tiercel Goshawk. Very often the Harris Hawk is compared with the Goshawk by falconers in terms of speed and tenacity when hunting. The comparison is an unfair one as they are totally different in the way in which they hunt in the wild.

led me to appreciate the hunting companionship of several more of my own Harris Hawks and plenty of hunting experiences with other people's.

This success with the species has prompted me to travel abroad and see them flown in many different terrains at various quarry species. It has also sufficiently fired my enthusiasm to make me want to see them in action in the wild and fly at least one passage example. The latter is an experience I enjoyed greatly and will undoubtedly try and repeat as soon as circumstances allow.

The Harris Hawk has earnt itself a very special place in the annuls of modern falconry and it is a place that I think is well deserved. It is a very biddable hawk that hunts well and is an extremely pleasant companion.

chapter two

equipment

Furniture is the equipment needed by the hawk and the falconer to enable them to carry out their sport. Some of the items are thousands of years old in terms of design, although modern materials may well have replaced those used by our ancestors. As a reader you may well want to skip this chapter as most of what is going to be said here you probably will already be aware of and will wish to move on to save yourself getting bored. If it is any consolation to you imagine if it is boring to read just how tedious do you think it is to write?

The first consideration to be given to the pending arrival of a new hawk is its housing and somewhere to weather it. This is dealt with in detail in the following chapter. A supply of hawk food comes next and somewhere to keep it. Wives seem to have a strange aversion for some reason to boxes of chicks, quail, mice, rats and the occasional rabbit being put in the freezer along with the household food. So it is probably best to get a separate freezer for your hawk food. As to a source, there are various commercial suppliers around these days whose products are first class and so is their delivery service. Long gone are the days when a falconer would have to scratch around trying to keep his hawks supplied with decent food out of the hawking season.

Next, let's deal with the furniture relating directly to the hawk. Firstly will be the anklets and jesses. Nowadays the Aylmeri system is the norm and traditional jesses are a thing of the past. The best quality jesses are made from Kangaroo skin and I personally use those that have been made from a skin cured by the vegetable tanning process. With the Aylmeri system the anklet stays permanently in place and depending on the circumstances either mews or field jesses are fitted. Mews Jesses have a button at one end to prevent them being pulled through the anklet and a slit at the other end to allow them to be attached to the swivel. Field jesses are the same in design except that they do not have a slit for attaching to the swivel. The idea is that if a hawk is flown with field jesses fitted she does not run the risk of getting hooked up by the slit, no matter how small that risk may be. I always have at least two pairs of mews jesses on the go for a hawk at any given time. This way I can change them regularly, at least once a week, inspect them for wear and re-grease them. Decent jess grease is essential and I always use Ko-Cho-Line. It is a little messy to use but certainly does its job well.

There are also permanent flying jesses which are attached by means of the eyelet to the anklet. These tend to be longer and thinner than normal jesses and are fitted for the entire duration of the flying season. Then there is the bullet jess arrangement. This is a system of

Adult female Harris Hawk in flight clearly showing a tail mounted telemetry transmitter and permanent flying jesses.

quick fit and removal of jesses that are attached permanently to the swivel. Instead of a button at the opposite end to the swivel there is a metal toggle button which is pushed through the eyelet and then turned sideways to prevent it slipping back through. Some bullet jess systems have a collar which can then be pushed up against the eyelet to ensure the bar cannot possibly come back through. They are normally only used when out in the field and are replaced by more conventional Aylmeri once back home. I personally do not use the bullet jess system on Harris Hawks as I have seen accidents involving their use on two separate occasions. I fully realize that many people use them on a daily basis and have probably never experienced any problem with them, but the fault I saw happen twice was the same fault and only quick thinking on one of the occasions prevented a hawk being killed because of it.

Next comes the swivel. These vary in shape and size and you should use whatever you are most comfortable with. The idea of a swivel is to prevent the jesses or leash becoming entangled by allowing both components to be able to move freely without restricting the movement of each other. I personally prefer what is known as the flat top design of swivel as I feel that the slit end of the jess is less likely to slip down the body of the swivel and thereby prevent its free movement. Also the flat top design helps the two ends of the jesses lock against each other and keep them neat as well as out of harm's way. Whatever design of swivel you decide to go for please ensure that it is made from stainless steel or titanium and

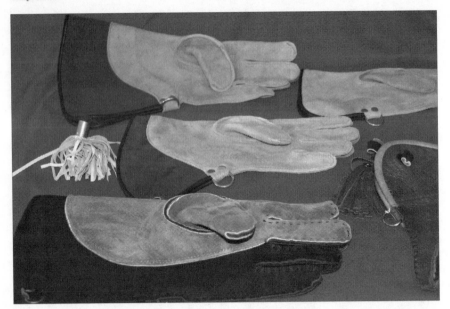

Gloves. Normally a single thickness for a male Harris Hawk and a double thickness for a female. The best gloves are Elk or Buckskin and will last for years if looked after properly.

is from a reputable source. There are many very cheap swivels on the market and none were originally designed to withstand the bating of a hawk. Equipment is one of the areas where under no circumstances whatsoever, should the falconer ever try and cut corners or save a few pounds. A small accident can result in the death or serious injury of a hawk. Better to spend a little more and have complete confidence in the equipment you use.

A small point to remember is that when you are passing the ends of the jesses through the main body of the swivel before bringing them back up and over to attach them securely, make sure you push the second jess through the way the point of the first one ended. That will mean when you pull the second one up it will finally settle the opposite way to the first and not only will this look neater and be less of a bulky mess but one jess will also lock the other in place. Do not do, as I have seen done quite a lot lately, put both jesses through together and pull them up the same way. They do not stay in position like this and inevitably one or both slide down the main body of the swivel and stop it functioning correctly.

After the swivel comes the leash. Nowadays modern materials have replaced the leather leash and a great many hawks are still alive due to that fact. Leather leashes were very effective but needed to be constantly scrutinized and oiled to ensure they were not wearing through. Many a hawk has been lost because a sudden bate caused a leash to part at the button end. Again do not be tempted to use cheap materials for your leashes. Polypropylene does not make for good leashes and hawks can pick at the leash and get strands of it to lift. There is a danger that not only can they eat through the leash but can also ingest strands of the material they have picked. Despite the fact that modern materials are now used almost

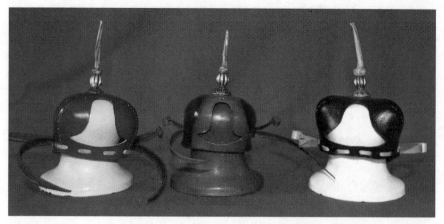

A selection of hoods on hood blocks. From left to right they are a blocked anglo-indian, a dutch pattern and an ordinary anglo-indian. Most falconers tend to use the ordinary anglo-indian as this is the pattern that most hawks seem to accept readily and obviously find comfortable.

exclusively, still make it a point to check leashes on a regular basis. Ensure that there are no weak spots particularly round the button end and that the hawk is not picking constantly at a particular place.

Most falconers still put bells on their hawks and not just as location aids when out hawking. Bells can be very useful at home, their ringing will tell a falconer if a hawk is merely scratching or perhaps having a bath. They will also signify if a hawk is restless or if something has alarmed it. For those that care to listen the whole range of signals is there. Also, of course, in the field bells are a very valuable aid to the falconer. Before telemetry they were the main weapon in the falconers armoury for locating a lost hawk, albeit temporarily. The sound would also warn the falconer if a hawk was on the move or struggling with quarry.

Bells are attached to the hawk by several means. The traditional way is by leather bewits and these come in two forms. The traditional bewit is a very thin strip of leather that, through a cunning arrangement of three holes, fastens a bell directly to the leg of the hawk. The button bewit is again a thin strip of leather but instead of a series of holes has a button one end and a slit the other. The button can be passed through the slit after the body of the bewit has been passed around the leg of the hawk. The difference between this and the traditional bewit is that the button bewit can be quickly removed or refitted as required. Some falconers prefer that when their hawk is not in the field the bells should be silent. Button bewits are one method of achieving this but so is slipping a pre-cut slither of cardboard into the slit in the bell. When the hawk is taken up again to fly, the cardboard is simply pulled out.

A bell can also be mounted on the tail and this is very effective as a hawk, particularly when out hunting, moves its tail a great deal. The bell can be mounted on the tail by numerous methods. There is a cable tie that comes with a small circular attachment at one end that has a hole though it. The cable tie is attached to a deck feather and then the bell attached to it, by means of a much smaller cable tie. The bell can also be mounted on a plectrum which is then

Two adult male Harris Hawks on high perches.

attached to the deck feathers. Or, it can be mounted by means of a specially adapted telemetry tail mount that has provision for a bell as well as a transmitter.

A bell can also be put around the hawk's neck by means of an elastic band. It goes without saying that the elastic band should be a weak one and break if it meets with any resistance. There are those that condemn this method out of hand and say that its usage is simply asking for trouble. But I must say I have never encountered a problem with it nor have I ever had a hawk even remotely inconvenienced by it, let alone being injured.

There are those that cable tie a bell to the anklet of the hawk and personally I think this is a sloppy practice and one that ends up making the anklet bulky, but it is probably not dangerous to the hawk. A method that is thoroughly stupid and simply inviting a serious injury to take place is using a cable tie to attach a bell directly to the hawk's leg. This is so stupid and blatantly dangerous as to need no explanation why. But I have seen this method used on many occasions and whenever I speak to those that practice this they seem oblivious to any harm that could result from it.

Another item that is generally placed on the tail of the hawk is the telemetry transmitter mount. Again, these come in various forms the most common being a brass tube that is

Adult male Harris Hawk on a high perch.

clamped to a deck feather by means of elongated sides fitted to it. The deck feather is cleared of feathers as high up as can be reached easily and then the tail mount is fitted by squeezing the sides around the deck feather shaft, having already coated them with impact adhesive on the surface that will make contact with the quill as well.

Another piece of equipment worn by the hawk is the hood. This is dealt with in great detail in the chapter on hooding. Hooding a hawk is such an important part of its training and so often only referred to in passing or skipped over all together that I felt the item itself and its usage merited a separate chapter.

Having equipped the hawk we now need something for it to perch on. Depending on whether the hawk is loose in an aviary, tethered in a weathering or out on a lawn there are several viable options. If the hawk is loose in an aviary then the perches can either be branches or shelf perches. The shelf perch is a semi circular plastic shelf with a raised lip around its top edge that is designed to retain a piece of artificial grass. The size of the perch will vary depending on where you purchase your falconry equipment from. For Harris Hawks I use perches that have a twelve inch radius. This is more than large enough for the hawk to perch comfortably on.

Falconer wearing a hawking vest instead of the traditional hawking bag. An extremely versatile garment and one that is less likely to catch going over fences.

Tethered in a weathering I much prefer a hawk to again sit on a shelf perch. There are those that argue that shelf perches cause feather damage to the primary feathers of the hawk and are more trouble than they are worth. I would suggest that those who think like this should pay more attention to the manning process of their hawk. A hawk that is restless and is constantly flitting from the ground to the perch and back again will indeed rub its feathers against the back of the weathering to which the shelf perch is attached, but should a hawk that is not yet fully manned be tethered in a weathering anyway? Once a hawk is properly manned it will sit quietly in its weathering and I believe a shelf perch offers it the most comfort without risk of any damage to its feet or feathers.

There are some hawks that do not like shelf perches and these are better off on the more conventional bow perch. I myself have two male Harris Hawks that are brothers. One is happiest on a bow, the other on a shelf and so their weatherings are equipped accordingly. There is no hard and fast rule on perching other than it should be safe and not inclined to induce foot problems in the hawk.

When it comes to bow perches there are several combinations to choose from. Firstly, there are indoor bow perches; these are equipped with very heavy feet instead of spikes that you have to push into the ground. As their name implies they are for use when it is required to perch a hawk indoors – very useful for when you are away from home hawking. Secondly, the outdoor bow has the spikes for pushing into the ground instead of the heavy feet. Nowadays many people don't bother with the outdoor type and use the indoor for both purposes. This is okay unless the perch does not have heavy enough feet to prevent the perch sliding when a hawk bates from it. You will be surprised just how much a hawk can drag an indoor bow, particularly on wet grass. I have known of more than one hawk killed in just such a way. It really cannot be stressed too much that the weight of the feet really does have to be quite considerable to prevent the hawk being able to shift the perch, that is why I prefer to have both types. It only requires a relatively small outlay in terms of pounds to have complete peace of mind.

The material that the actual perching area of the bow is covered in, presents the falconer with several options. The more usual are either leather, artificial grass or rubber. Some people use rope which is okay and some use polypropylene which is definitely not, for exactly the same reason as it should not be used for leashes. I use either leather or rubber. Of the two I prefer leather which is placed on top of a sheet foam foundation. This has 'give' for the hawk's feet but has the disadvantage that it wears quickly if used in outside conditions and is not that easy to keep clean properly.

A further perching option is the high perch. This is a relatively new type of perch, or to be more accurate the reworking of a type of perch that has been around for a long time in Germany but not used much here. It consists of a slender column of plastic some three foot high and approximately six inches in diameter. It is capped on the top and the bottom is welded to a circular disc some two foot in diameter and a quarter of an inch thick to produce a sturdy base. The tube then has a four inch diameter hole drilled into it a foot or so down from the top with a one inch hole just above it. The cap on the top is covered in artificial grass and has a quarter of an inch hole drilled down through it so as to enable a leash to be threaded down from the top and taken out through the larger of the two holes in the side. The leash can then be fastened securely by passing it between the large and small holes and tying loose hitches between them. Providing the swivel is kept tight to the cap this will mean the hawk has only the length of its jesses as its movement. Before the hawk is put on and then attached to the perch the central column can be filled with water or sand to give it stability.

I have modified the design of this type of perch to better suit my own needs. For example, mine are four foot high instead of three and I have the bottom part of the central column capped as well as the top. Then I have a detachable base plate made up that has a 10 inch high piece of tube welded to its centre that has an inner circumference just fractionally larger than the outer circumference of the column. This tube is then strengthened with four additional short wing-like stabilizers. The removable base means the perch is extremely easy to transport, something which can be a problem with the fixed base type. The reason I have gone for the increase in height is that I find my hawks prefer being that little bit higher.

I was slow in giving these perches a try initially but now I have I find them superb. Hawks

Telemetry transmitter fitted to the tail of an adult female Harris Hawk.

like them because they are well up off of the ground and don't find everything else around them quite so threatening because of it. This is particularly true when it comes to dogs. In the case of a hawk that has not seen dogs before or one that has shown a dislike for them this perching system is ideal for getting it to accept their presence. Whilst the hawk is on its perch the dog, or dogs, can mill around and because the hawk is above them it is not so ill at ease. The same hawk low down on a bow perch would be feeling extremely threatened and this would re-inforce any fear or hatred it had of dogs. In fact a friend of mine has a hawk that has never been happy with dogs anywhere near it. We set about trying to cure its dislike with the aid of a high perch.

The hawk was dropped off each day by my friend as he passed my house on his way to work and on his way home in the evening he would collect it again. In the interval the hawk would have spent the day on a high perch in my garden with my four dogs. At first only one dog was in the same part of the garden as the hawk although it could see the other three, not too far away, at all times. When the hawk's behaviour indicated it was not worried by the dog being around it anymore another dog was added to equation. This continued until all four dogs would be around the hawk all day and their presence was hardly noticed. This particular hawk now hunts well over my dogs although it does not get to work with them more than two or three times a month.

Another advantage I have found is that when I hawk away from home the mobility and flexibility of the perches means they can be used as an indoor perch as well if so required. Sometimes when you rent a cottage in Scotland, or wherever, for some rabbit hawking not a lot of consideration has been given to accommodating the hawks. High perches tend to help overcome any such shortcomings. Also, if you put your hawks out to weather on a conventional bow perch and the ground is damp it takes just one bate for wing and tail tips to be soaked. A bate from the high perch gives no such problems. All in all I am very impressed with the system, especially my adapted version.

Transporting the hawk from home to hunting ground or for a visit to the vets is best accomplished by using a travelling box. These used to be made of wood which had the disadvantages of being heavy and difficult to keep clean. Also, if they were scrubbed out in an effort to clean them thoroughly the wood absorbed a certain amount of water and they remained damp for some considerable time. Nowadays, transport boxes are made of man-made materials which are both considerably lighter in weight, incredibly strong, easier to keep clean and are also generally far more durable than their wooden predecessors.

There can be no question that the use of transport boxes instead of cadges and travelling bow perches have saved many damaged feathers and many hawks' lives. If you travel several hawks together and use transport boxes then each hawk is individually cocooned and cannot hurt or be hurt by another hawk. When buying such a box look for a few basic refinements. The base should be recessed so as to give stability when travelling. The door should close onto a rebated panel and the fittings should be stainless steel. Mine have anti shake catches and are fitted so that they open by moving the catch 90° up, not down. In this way it isn't physically possible for the catch to come undone and the door open by mistake. When cleaning use a viricidal disinfectant and rinse thoroughly.

Another item that is made from modern materials, such as plastic or fibre glass, is the hawk bath. This is now an item that is easily purchased from any falconry furniture supplier and is designed specifically for the job. No longer is there the need to mess around with odd trays from garden centres or up-turned dustbin lids. Most modern hawk baths are some 26 to 30 inches in diameter, approximately four inches deep and have sloping sides to enable the hawk to sit comfortably on the rim before stepping in. The floor of the bath is ribbed so that the hawk can grip once she is in the bath. A bath will hold around two gallons of water and this should be changed each time the hawk is offered a bath.

A further piece of equipment that has not found general favour in Britain but is used in many other countries is the hunting T perch. These tend to be popular with those that fly a cast of Harris Hawks together. This is a pole some five or six feet long that has a T piece of approximately 18 inches attached to one end and this extra limb is covered with artificial grass. The hawk, when fully trained, is encouraged to return as freely to the T perch as it is to the fist. When hawking in long grass or dense ground cover the hawk can be encouraged to get on the T perch and the perch is then held aloft by the falconer. This gives the hawk an additional height advantage as opposed to sitting on the fist. That little bit of extra height can make all the difference, the hawk can spot an item of prey moving around in the cover.

I have used one just for the sake of experimentation and have to admit the result can be quite effective. But as I do not like flying more than one Harris Hawk at any one time and I prefer my hawk to be flown from the fist I have no real desire to use such a perch in my hawking. But for those that do fly hawks in a group or by the following on method then the perch does have advantages that make its use worthwhile.

An essential item for the hawk house is a set of accurate scales on which to weigh the hawk daily. These can be either of the balance type or electronic, but whatever type you decide to buy, make sure that you get the best quality that you can afford. They need to be accurate and reliable. Electronic scales used to have so many stupid myths and falsehoods attached to them that a lot of people would not use them. Inaccuracies such as if the battery was getting low the weight would be less than it really was. Another, was that electronic scales were not accurate enough for weighing a hawk daily. Needless to say this is utter rubbish and electronic scales are extremely accurate, down to tiny amounts. Most have a switch so that you can choose to weigh in metric or imperial and if the battery is getting low the scales themselves will tell you by either indicating low battery or showing error.

For training the hawk you need a creance, lure and whistle. The creance is an extremely long line, which is wrapped around a turned piece of wood. The length of the creance is normally around 50 metres and should not have any form of spring clip fitted to the free end. The creance should be attached to the slits in the mews jesses not the swivel when in use. The use of the creance will be gone into more fully in the training chapter.

Hawks are trained primarily to the fist but it is always a good idea to train them to a lure as well so as to give yourself a back up. The traditional lure for a Harris Hawk would normally be a rabbit lure. You can use a bird-based lure as you would for a falcon, it really does not make any difference to the hawk. The only thing that matters to it is that the lure represents food and if the hawk comes to it then it is sure of a reward. It used to be considered of prime importance

Adult female Harris Hawk on a leather topped stainless steel outdoor bow perch. Beside her is a modern custom made hawk bath.

that a hawk chased a dragged rabbit lure for all it was worth before it could be taken out into the field to chase a real rabbit. This really isn't crediting the hawk with very much sense. Even an extremely realistic rabbit lure does not look or run like a rabbit. Resorting to dragging a dead example of the real thing does not really teach a hawk to follow the twists and turns of the rabbit when it is running for its life. A lure is really only an additional recall method that the falconer has up his sleeve for recovering his hawk. It doesn't really matter what you use for a lure as long as it is consistent and the hawk knows it signifies food for them.

The hawk is taught to return to the glove when the falconer calls, whistles or holds his fist aloft, or any combination of the three. I find it a good idea to use a football referee's whistle to call the hawk as this can carry a great deal further than my own whistle. An Acme Thunderer is the most readily available and is without doubt one of the loudest whistles on the market.

There is little doubt that the most expensive outlay a falconer will have to make, other than the hawk itself, is telemetry. This is the radio tracking system which is an aid to locating a lost hawk or dog. The receiver is a relatively straightforward affair that picks up a radio signal from a small transmitter fitted to the hawk and in most cases the falconer's dog. It normally comes with a fold flat aerial and slips neatly into a carrying case that can be carried on the falconer's back without too much hindrance. There are even some extremely neat sets that will, quite literally, slip in your pocket. The hawk is fitted with a small and very light transmitter that will give off a detectable signal for a considerable range. Most transmitters nowadays weigh between four and six grams, even when the batteries are fitted. Such a slight weight does not hinder the hawk in anyway providing the transmitter is fitted sensibly.

When mounting the transmitter there are several practical options. Probably the most usual is a small brass tube which is glued to a deck feather as high up as possible and the transmitter is fitted into it by means of a spring clip. But they can also be neck mounted with an elastic band, as mentioned with bells earlier. They can be mounted on the leg by means of a button bewit or they can be mounted on the back with what's known as a back pack kit. This is a relatively new idea and involves passing a cleverly designed tape around the hawks chest and across its back which is then sewn together and a mount for the telemetry sits neatly high up in the centre of the hawk's back. When the transmitter is mounted into the tube it is completely out of the way and almost impossible for it to get caught up on anything. I personally have only used this system on small falcons but intend to expand its use in the future. When used in conjunction with a transmitter that can be switched on and off with a magnet, then the normal practice is to leave the transmitter in place for the season, only taking it off to change batteries.

Do not be tempted to mount a transmitter to the leg of the hawk by means of a cable tie, this is inviting a serious accident. If you really must use cable ties then attach them to the eyelet in the Aylmeri anklet. But it really does take so little time or effort to put a mount on the tail of the hawk or use a button bewit that there really is no need or excuse for using cable ties.

Transmitters are now available for dogs and it makes sense to use them. They do more than simply help with location of the dog in thick cover. Most dog transmitters on the market give off two separate signals. One will indicate that the dog is stationary, the other that it is

Freda, my pointer fitted with a telemetry transmitter collar. Note the heavy buckle which helps keep the aerial in the upright position. This collar transmitter is switched on by passing a magnet across it.

moving. I started using these on the grouse moors where dogs have to run great distances in order to find birds and are often out of sight. They may be down in a peat hag or over a ridge. But with the transmitter in place it is possible to know whether or not they are on point without having to go over the ridge to have a look. Also, we live nowadays in times where dogs are stolen all too often. To have a transmitter on the dog is a good idea and most of those on the market come as an integral part of a special collar.

Just like the latest hawk transmitters they can be turned on and off with a magnet and the collar is specially weighted so that the short stubby aerial is always in the upright position. I use them all the time and wouldn't run one of my dogs without one. The cost of a collar transmitter is only around the same as a two stage transmitter for a hawk, so it really is a good investment and, looked after properly, will literally last for years.

If you hawk with friends on a regular basis then it makes sense that you all operate your telemetry on the same wave length so that should something go wrong you can all help one another in locating the lost hawk or dog. Again, if several friends are going to hawk together on a regular basis then any newcomer to their group can just initially buy a transmitter that

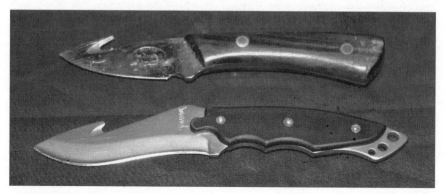

Knives with gralloching hooks.

will be picked up on their sets. Then a little later on purchase a compatible receiver.

Do not make the common mistake of thinking telemetry is a magic box that guarantees recovery of a lost hawk. What it will do, if all goes well, is lead you to the errant hawk, whether or not you then get it back is another matter. Don't be tempted to take on flights that you have serious doubts about just because telemetry is fitted. Also, ensure that you know your set well and are capable of accurately interpreting the signals it gives off to you. All too often people use their telemetry for the first time when they actually need to track down their hawk. Take your time and get to know your set before you have to use it for real. Get someone to hide a transmitter for you and then track it down. Learn the sort of things that can give you a bounced signal and how to work out that you are in fact getting a bounced signal. The more you play with the set the better you will know it.

In your hawk house you will need a basic tool kit for jobs relating to the hawk. This will include things like a leather punch, eyelet tool, eyelets, scalpel, metal ruler, cutting board and of course some leather for jesses, etc. You will also need a coping set for trimming the hawk's beak and talons as and when required

The falconer will also require a glove. Like all equipment, buy the best quality products and look after them. Falconry equipment is like anything else in life, you get what you pay for. Get the best you can afford, it will pay in the long run. For a male Harris Hawk a single thickness glove will suffice but a female will require a double. The best gloves are made from buck or elk skin and are extremely strong as well as being soft and supple. Make sure they are treated with a decent brand of leather dressing when new and each season take the time and trouble to clean them properly and re-treat them with dressing. I have a glove I have been using for 16 years now and it is still going strong.

A falconry bag was the traditional way that falconers carried all the paraphernalia they needed when out in the field as well as any quarry taken. Nowadays these have been all but replaced by the hawking waistcoat or vest. I personally prefer the vest as it has greater flexibility in its usage and is a sturdier garment, but this is purely a matter of taste.

A decent knife is a valuable tool and I like those that have a small gralloching hook as part of the blade. These make either gutting or skinning the rabbit or hare extremely quick and easy with the absolute minimum of mess. I never buy expensive knives though as it is all too easy to leave one stuck in the ground somewhere. The other thing I do on my knives is to completely destroy the cutting edge of the blade with the exception of the last half inch or so. I take the knife to a grinding wheel and round off the sharp side of the blade. That way I cannot suffer the type of accident I have known happen to two other people where the hawk has grabbed the blade of the knife whilst the falconer was dispatching the rabbit.

chapter three
housing

Before the arrival of the hawk it goes without saying that its housing should be complete and ready to receive it. Various considerations will need to be taken into account with regard to sighting and dimensions. Most people will have to make any hawk accommodation fit in with an already existing garden as opposed to starting with a blank piece of paper and building the ideal set-up. What will be required are a weathering and/or an aviary. Also an area where the hawk can be put out to weather in safety from any stray dogs, cats, foxes or children.

When the hawk first arrives it is best kept in a weathering tethered to a bow perch or shelf perch. Ensure that the leash is not tied too long as this can result in serious injuries to the hawk's legs. The mistake that many beginners make is to try and give the hawk maximum possible length on the leash thinking they are being kind to the hawk. In actual fact the opposite is true and the hawk is put at risk every time it bates if the leash is sufficiently long to allow it to attain full acceleration. When it is fully trained and is not prone to crashing around when loose then it can be housed in an aviary. If it is not possible to have a weathering and an aviary then just an aviary will suffice. The hawk can be tethered to a bow in the aviary during its training, providing of course all higher perches have been removed. If not then the poor hawk will spend all its time trying in vain to reach the higher vantage point. Any aviary or weathering needs to be sighted so that the prevailing wind does not blow directly into it. It should also offer the hawk the opportunity of enjoying the morning sun whilst shading it from the extreme heat of the day. Provision must also be made to allow the hawk to shelter from the rain if it so desires. Many hawks enjoy sitting out in the rain and will often prefer to do so, even in quite heavy showers, but if they have the provision of shelter then at least the choice is theirs and not one that has been foisted on them.

Don't forget to take into account vermin when planning your construction work for housing your hawk. Foxes, rats and mink, if you live by water, are an everyday fact of life even if you live in built-up areas. Put your building on a wall of breeze blocks that itself sits on a concrete base. This way foxes will not be able to dig down and get into the aviary or weathering. If this is not possible in your situation then dig down at least a foot lower into the ground than you want the floor level to be at when you are finished. Then put down a wire base before putting the pea shingle on top of it. This will stop rats burrowing up from underneath but will not affect the drainage when you hose out the facility. Also, run wire down into the ground for a decent depth from the sides, this will stop foxes digging their way in.

Adult male Harris Hawk in a weathering that is equipped with a bow perch and pea shingle as a base material. Also note the clear plastic sheeting screwed to the wall behind so as to enable the area to be cleaned easily.

When building a weathering or aviary always try and build larger than required as opposed to down to the minimum requirement. A weathering that will be suitable for either a male or a female Harris Hawk will be approximately eight foot deep, eight foot wide and five foot high at the front sloping to four feet nine inches at the back. The sides, back and roof will be solid with the front section covered in one-inch square twiweld. Half the width of the front will be an outward opening door and the roof should also be covered with good quality roofing felt. The seams of the felt can be painted with one of the bitumen products on the market to ensure that it is thoroughly waterproof. Also, sealing down the seams means that winds are unlikely to prize any edges up and then tear them.

Adult male Harris Hawk

What I also do in my weatherings is fit clear plastic sheeting round the bottom half of the back and both sides. This plastic is the flat as opposed to corrugated type and comes in sheets six foot long by two foot wide by quarter of an inch thick. The sheets themselves are reasonably easy to cut to length and I fix them so that the plastic protects the wood of the weathering for the first two feet up from the floor. I then put a clear sealant around every edge to stop water getting in between the plastic and the wood. If a hawk slices sufficiently far to hit one of the walls of the weathering it is a simple matter to hose the messy area down.

A perch for the hawk will be required and either a traditional bow perch or a shelf perch can be utilised. In the early stages in the training of the hawk, in my opinion, a bow perch is probably better. The hawk will be more inclined to bate at this stage and a shelf perch will mean it is constantly brushing the back wall of the shelter and its wing tips will no doubt suffer accordingly. Once the manning process has produced a calm hawk that will sit quietly then the bow can be removed and a shelf perch fitted. This will be placed in the middle of the back wall approximately two feet from the ground. The semi-circular shelf perch is covered with astro turf and hawks seem to find them very comfortable. Screwed into the frame of the back section of the wall will be a retaining ring directly in line with the middle of the perch and just above ground level. I always use the large screw eyes that are readily available from most DIY stores. They cost around £1.00 each and if screwed in properly are impossible for a hawk to pull out. This will be for the attachment of the leash.

Shelf perches have several advantages. Firstly, a hawk sitting on one slices away from the

An adult male Harris Hawk in a weathering that has a shelf perch fitted. Not all hawks find this type of perching arrangement to their liking but most are happy on it. There are those that say this perching system causes hawks to damage their own feathers by rubbing them on the wall behind them. This is only the case with poorly manned or extremely restless hawks in which case the bow perch or another alternative can be used.

walls out into the middle of the weathering, thereby keeping its surroundings much cleaner. Properly installed it is more or less impossible for a hawk to become in any way entangled with or across the shelf. The fact that the astro turf is removable and the base structure is plastic means that the whole unit is easy to keep thoroughly cleaned. I have a spare astro turf inner cut ready for each of my shelf perches, which means I can change them over every week.

There are those that decry the use of shelf perches and even go so far as to suggest that their usage almost certainly guarantees the occupant having primaries that are worn down and a damaged tail. All I can say is that I have used them for a good many years and to the best of my knowledge have not suffered so much as a quarter of an inch of a damaged feather as a result Their use is most certainly inappropriate for an unmanned, unhooded hawk or falcon – constant bating against a hard surface that has no give in it will cause feather damage. However, for well manned hawks shelf perches are ideal. I tend to be very sceptical of anything new and I'm relatively resistant to change, the system has actually been around a lot longer than we tend to give it credit for. The American falconer Dr. Heinz Meng was using it some 30 years ago. Nevertheless, through personal experience, I have gone over almost entirely to this system and certainly advocate its use in nearly all cases. I have known falcons in the past that were very restless, despite being well manned and thoroughly trained, and these would probably have damaged their flight feathers on shelf perches, so obviously in their cases an alternative method would be used.

The floor of the weathering can be covered with either silver sand or pea shingle. Both have advantages and disadvantages but my own personal preference is for pea shingle. The big disadvantage of pea shingle is that if you have a hawk that is restless or poorly manned then the small stones are very abrasive to the tips of the feathers, but then a hawk that is not manned properly should not be left unhooded in a weathering.

I prefer pea shingle to sand because it is easy to keep clean and hawks occasionally pick it up and swallow it. Deliberately giving several small stones for a hawk to swallow is known as giving rangle and the stones themselves help to clean the inside of the crop by removing the build up of fatty material. The hawk casts the stones back up and this helps to bring some of this unpleasant material out. In Falconry, being the sport it is, there's even a special name for this fatty grease, and that is Gleam. But more Gleam will also be passed out the other end as it has been disturbed by the agitation of the stones and then taken down further into the system with the food the hawk has eaten. Rangle used to be an intricate part of reconditioning a hawk after the moult, but appears not to be widely used nowadays. All hawks benefit from taking rangle now and then, no matter what time of the year, and so much the better if they do it voluntarily. Simon Latham wrote almost 400 years ago that 'Washed meat and stones maketh a hawk to fly but great casting and much fasting maketh her to die'. The observation is nonetheless true now than it was all those years ago.

Silver sand is also abrasive to wingtips but not to the extent that shingle is, but it can get lodged in the scales on the hawk's feet and has been known to trigger an infection on more than one occasion. It can, of course, also be ingested. Another disadvantage in my mind is that sand becomes messy and claggy once a hawk has muted across it. Whereas shingle can be thoroughly cleaned by means of a hose or, better still, a pressure washer, sand has to be sifted to get the really soiled bits out. Accordingly this means it also has to be topped up regularly.

One thing that has to also be included in any structure that houses a hawk nowadays is a decent lock. Unfortunately we live in degenerate times where there are a few people who are happy to steal a hawk, either to fly it themselves or sell it for some imaginary inflated price.

In my experience I have found that suitable dimensions for an aviary will be as follows. Eight foot high at the front sloping to seven foot nine inches at the rear. Width will be eight feet and the depth 12 feet. Again the roof and back are better off being solid with one or both of the sides and the front being covered in one-inch square twiweld. One inch square may seem rather a fine mesh for such a large hawk, but unfortunately I know of two separate cases where foxes have killed the occupant of larger meshed aviaries by literally pulling them, or bits of them, through the mesh. The roof should be treated in the same way as with the weathering to ensure that it is thoroughly waterproof and resistant to being ripped off by excessively strong winds. Please note that these dimensions are purely for a one-hawk aviary. Its use is designed for a single hawk that is either being flown or is turned loose to moult. The dimensions given are also minimum measurements but, within reason, bigger is better.

Depending on the nature of the individual hawk it may be necessary to place vertical bars on the inside of the twiweld mesh of the aviary. Some hawks are extremely restless and fly against the wire and then hang on causing considerable damage to their tail feathers. These hawks tend to be the exception but it is worth making the provision for fitting such bars when carrying out the original aviary construction. There may also be external factors that influence whether or not you fit vertical bars. For example, a very good friend of mine has a very calm and laid back female Harris Hawk. But his garden appears to be the neighbourhood gathering place for the local frog population at certain times of the year. When his hawk sees this food source parading in front of her aviary she tries to get at them and could damage her cere on the wire if it were not for the bars. The bars themselves can either be bamboo or something like three quarter inch doweling. They should be spaced just close enough together to stop the hawk being able to make direct contact with the wire, at the same time making sure they are far enough apart to allow the maximum amount of light still being able to penetrate the aviary.

The aviary will again be equipped with shelf perches and perches made from branches covered with astro turf. These are normally placed across the corners where hawks often like to sit. Another thing that Harris Hawks in particular seem to like is a swing perch. This is a branch type perch suspended by means of a rope at each end from the roof of the aviary. Each time the hawk lands on the perch it will rock back and forth for a while. This is motion that many hawks seem to enjoy.

No tethering rings will be required, for obvious reasons, but a bath will and positioning the bath will probably be by trial and error till you find a patch that the hawk does not slice on. It is also advisable to site it so that you can flush it out and re-fill it without having to repeatedly go in to the aviary. A safety porch around the door is a good idea as countless hawks have been lost as they make a dash past their keepers when a door is half open. A simple safety porch covered with something like pheasant pen netting is very cheap, easy to construct and most of all safe. Again, the floor of the aviary can be covered with either sand or pea shingle. My preference is, as with the weathering, for the shingle because of the ease with which it can be kept clean.

With the use of either the weathering or the aviary you will still require an area to actually weather the hawk in. This may seem a strange thing to say when the hawk is secure in its weathering or free to move around in the aviary. The reason to bring the hawk out of either and put it out on a bow is more to keep it disciplined as opposed to anything else. No matter how well manned a hawk is and no matter how well it flies it can get a little above itself if it is taken straight out of its housing to be flown. It is better to take the hawk out, weigh it and set it down to weather for an hour or so before taking it out to hunt. Also, any hawk kept in an aviary for any length of time will get territorial and so it is imperative that you remain in charge and bring the hawk out each day and make sure the weathering area affords the hawk some shade from the midday and early afternoon sun.

Whilst out on the bow the hawk can also be given the opportunity to bathe if it has not to your certain knowledge done so recently. If you use dogs as hunting companions then it does no harm for the hawk and dog to see each other at close quarters before going out to enjoy your sport.

An item not to be forgotten when working out what construction you will have to do to accommodate your new hawk will be a hawk room for scales, freezer and all the other equipment you will need for the well being of the hawk. As I said at the start of this chapter

Hawks on an indoor shelf perch arrangement in the hawk house at Thrumster Estates, northern Scotland. This is a way of keeping several hawks in the same room together as safely as possible. Each individual hawk cannot see or reach its neighbour.

most people will have to adapt and compromise with an existing set up. But make sure you do not compromise to the detriment of the safety or quality of life of the hawk.

One final consideration, which should be given to the sighting of any aviary or weathering, is that Harris Hawks are extremely intelligent and get bored very easily. Position their quarters where they see things going on around them. If you intend to use dogs and/or ferrets with your hawk then site the weathering, kennels and hutch so that they can all see each other. Don't tuck them away where they can only see a wall or a hedge. Also, I give my Harris Hawks toys to play with in the aviary when they are moulting. I use the plastic squeaky sort of toy you would give to a dog, but remove the squeaker from the bottom and give it to the hawk. They also appear to like tennis balls very much, but don't get the bright yellow ones that you can lift the material easily on. If you can lift it with your nail then a hawk can lift it a great deal more easily and possibly end up ingesting it.

Boredom should be avoided at all costs. Hawks that are bored can become vocal and they can also be prone to plucking out their own feathers and occasionally become extremely aggressive to anyone who enters their perceived territory. Should a hawk ever get like this then there is only one person to blame, and that is you.

Lighting is also desirable in the area of your weatherings and aviaries and I use the sort of system that comes on automatically when you pass in front of a sensor and break a beam. Apart from their practical use when you get home late from hunting or have to make an early start they might well act as a deterrent against foxes and also thieves.

What can be extremely useful is a cheap and cheerful monitoring system that can now be purchased from the larger DIY chains. They all seem to sell a mini camera system that you can plug into your television in the house. For around £30.00 you can keep an eye on your hawk without leaving the comfort of your front room and they are quite easy to install and almost maintenance free.

chapter four
hunting companions

F or the vast majority of falconers in the UK the appropriate hunting companions for the Harris Hawk will be dogs and ferrets. The roles of both these companion hunters are straightforward and of great assistance in obtaining flights for the hawk. Dogs are used to hunt, point and flush game, either fur or feather, and the breeds that are suitable for the job are many and varied. The role of the ferret is simply to bolt rabbits from the safety of their buries and present the hawk with a flight in the open.

There may be those that hunt from horseback with their hawks, but I don't have much experience of it. The two occasions I have tried, once with a Harris Hawk and once with falcons, did not inspire me sufficiently to want to try it again. Friends of mine in Mexico arranged for me to accompany two of them hunting in the desert with Harris Hawks from horseback. Because I love falconry, and always eager to try different branches of the sport, I happily went along. It was a male passage Harris that I was flying and he was not completely happy coming back to the fist whilst I was on the horse. So, each time he chased quarry and missed I would have to get off of the horse, then go through the process of hobbling it, walk some distance from it and then call the hawk back to the fist. Once the hawk was on the fist he would be hooded, the horse un-hobbled and then I would remount. If the horse and hawk had been a good deal more compatible then perhaps the experience would have been a far more enjoyable one, but they weren't and the dismounting and mounting routine became extremely tedious.

What probably also influenced me, with regard to horses, is my personal lack of riding skill and my mistrust of anything larger and more powerful than myself. I think that I will happily stick to dogs as part of my team and leave our equine friends to others.

Some will ask is a dog really necessary to ensure good sport with a hawk and isn't it possible to hawk well without one. You can hunt a Harris Hawk without the aid of a dog and the availability of quarry and the terrain it is found in will dictate how much hunting you will be able to do. But whatever the circumstances you will find many more flights with the aid of a good dog. To illustrate the point, I was hunting with some friends on an estate in Scotland some years back. Our party consisted of two female Red Tailed Hawks and two female Harris Hawks. One of the Red Tails would not tolerate the presence of dogs as it was around seven years old and had never worked with one, so the falconer concerned took his Red Tail to a promising looking part of the estate in search of rabbits. The rest of us went off and hawked over dogs and enjoyed a very successful morning.

When we all met up again in the early afternoon the lone Red Tail had not had a single

Hawking from horseback is not for me, although it is a good way to look for raptor nests in country unsuitable for vehicles.

flight despite being taken to several fields that had large patches of rough grass, reeds and marram grass. In fact the falconer concerned complained that there were probably no rabbits there at all and we had kept the best spot for ourselves. We all offered to go back with him and I would run a dog through the fields and see if we could get a rabbit flight for him. As his hawk would not tolerate the close proximity of a dog we positioned falconer and hawk on the far side of a likely looking patch and then, together with the pointer, made our way through it towards him. The idea was that if we flushed a rabbit it should break cover his side. The pointer came on point and we flushed a rabbit which the hawk promptly caught and killed. The pointer found another three rabbits in the same patch and another 11 in the next 40 minutes.

The same would be true in a copse or wood environment. It is so easy for game birds and rabbits to hide in cover, even from the incredible eyesight that hawks have. Providing they don't move they are relatively safe and they know that. But a dog with its superb nose will track them down for us – you will almost always find far more flights with a dog than without one. Not only that but if you are using one of the pointing breeds you will have pre-warning of the flight and therefore can get yourself and hawk into the most advantageous position.

When it comes to dogs there are a number of considerations to be taken into account when

Evie, a pointer that worked with hawks and falcons for 14 years and is now enjoying her retirement.

selecting a breed that is suitable to the hawking needs of the individual. For example, if a falconer only hawks ground quarry, and does not want to hunt game with falcons as well, then his choice will be different from the falconer that wishes to do both. The expression 'horses for courses' applies equally well when selecting a dog for your hawking needs. Let's take a quick look at the various breeds and discuss their different plus and minus points.

Pointers and Setters

The Pointer, often mistakenly referred to as The English Pointer, and the various Setter breeds are the classic dog of the open moorland. They have been bred specifically to cover large tracts of ground at high speed in pursuit of Red Grouse. The Pointer are very deep chested dogs and relatively lightly framed and are absolutely ideal for the job they were designed for. They seem to glide over the heather and are a joy to watch at work and I cannot think of many more stirring sights than seeing a Pointer or Setter running full tilt across a grouse moor then suddenly stopping dead and 'freezing' on a solid point. Once on point they will hold it for an astonishing amount of time if need be.

The Pointer, as we know it, was developed from the Spanish Pointer being crossed with the Old English Foxhound. It was the falconer and all round field sportsman Colonel Thornton who carried out the initial work in trying to obtain the sort of hunting dog he had in mind. Up until the 18th century Setters had been the primary game-locating dog in use in Great Britain. References have been found that relate to their usage as far back as the reign of Elizabeth 1 and with the increase in the popularity of the Pointer the use of Setters declined quite considerably. Although there have been some superb kennels of working Setters which have helped to keep the breed pure and as good at their job as ever they were. When it comes to running both breeds on the hill the only advantage I can see that the Pointer has over the Setter is that when the weather is very warm the short coat of the Pointer means it tires less easily.

Both Pointers and Setters will work well away from the moorland environment but they tend to over run the type of ground that will be covered by someone looking for a flight with a large hawk. The work rate of the Pointer or Setter is such that it is always having to be called back to keep it within a reasonable distance. Rabbits won't hold indefinitely to the point like many game birds and so the work rate of the pointer can turn out to be a disadvantage. It is no good if your Pointer finds rabbit after rabbit but too far away from you to give the hawk a decent chance.

My own circumstances are such that my passion in life is Grouse hawking with falcons, therefore I have Pointers and English Setters as my working dogs. Whenever I go out hawking with my Harris Hawk I take an old Pointer or Setter that the passage of time has slowed down. When working the moors gets to be too hard for them they enjoy a sort of semi retirement providing flights for my hawks instead of my falcons. Emma, an old favourite Pointer of mine, was still going out rabbit hawking to within weeks of her death at over 14 years old. I had tried hard to retire her completely and just let her rest out the last couple of years of her life, but she would have none of it. If she heard me loading up the hawks she became agitated and even more so when she realised she was being left behind, but even after she had a stroke she still came out two mornings a week. She was very slow by this time and we had to stop frequently to give her a rest. Despite her advanced age her nose was still as good as ever and the hawk trusted her completely.

Pointers and Setters are absolutely essential to me because of the fact I hunt Red Grouse with falcons, and if I didn't participate in this type of falconry then I have to admit I would seriously consider a different breed of dog to fly my Harris Hawks over.

German Short Haired Pointer

A medium sized, short coated dog from the Hunt, Point, Retrieve (HPR) family. They normally come in either liver and white or black and white, although occasionally you will come across solid liver or solid black examples. As a breed they have proven to be popular with both hawkers and shooting people alike. It is a relatively slow dog at covering the ground, by comparison to pointers and setters, but more than makes up for this by being extremely methodical. Normally willing to enter cover and water they are an extremely versatile breed with much to recommend them.

Freda the pointer has a rabbit marked down in a patch of marram grass.

German Wire Haired Pointer

This is another medium sized dog, but with a heavier frame than the short haired pointer and a very coarse wire coat. The breed is a relatively new one in recognised dog terms, being the result of specific cross breeding to obtain the desired result in the late 19th century. Michael Woodford had a photograph of a Wirehair in his *Manual of Falconry* which was published in 1960.

Falconers began taking an interest in the breed, but it was not for another 15 years or so that they were being bred regularly here in the United Kingdom. Foremost in establishing a good working bloodline in this country is the renowned falconer Diana Durman-Walters. One of her German Wirehair Pointer bitches won an open field trial on grouse as long ago as 1978. Diana still breeds first class dogs and flies her falcon over them on the moors each year and I have had the pleasure of seeing them work many times and they are extremely efficient at what they do.

It has to be said, that I have seen many others that are incredibly head strong and have to be dominated the whole time and they are a tough breed of dog designed to do a tough job in the stalking field and they are required to trail wounded deer and either hold them at bay or bring them back. Being far more used to the gentle nature of pointers and setters I find that GWP's are far too head strong for my liking but most of the falconers I know that use them for hawking swear by them.

Italian Bracco and Spinone

Both breeds are large heavy framed dogs designed for slow precise work. The Spinone is the wire haired version of the Bracco and their role in their working life is to find game, particularly on wetlands where scenting conditions can be difficult. They are heavy plodding dogs but first class swimmers but they are not used very much in this country – I've only seen them working in Italy.

Hungarian Vizla

A dog bred originally to do the same job as our setters, that is to locate game birds which would then be netted. Later it was gradually developed into a falconry and shooting dog by the Hungarian aristocracy. A medium sized, smooth coated dog which enjoys the most glorious russet colouring. As a breed they tend to be clever as well as obedient and almost pointer-like in the way they need to show and receive affection. Similar to pointers, they are quite sensitive and are easily spoilt by a heavy hand.

There is also a wire haired Vizla and this was evolved by selective crossing with German wire haired pointers.

Munsterlanders

There are two types of Munsterlander, the large and the small. Both are rather heavily built and tend to resemble either large setters or spaniels respectively. This is hardly surprising as both can be found in the breed's original make up. They are much slower than other breeds of pointing dogs at covering the ground but are very thorough, particularly in light cover.

When I lived in Austria I used one for my hawking and was very impressed with her. I flew a Goshawk at rabbits and pheasants over her as well as falcons at partridge, she coped with both situations admirably and she would go into water and flush ducks for a friend's peregrine falcon. As with most of the pointing breeds, Munsterlanders tend to be affectionate, very intelligent dogs and I would have thought them ideal for the dedicated Harris Hawker.

Brittanies

A French breed that for many years was mislabelled Brittany Spaniel. Although to be fair they are the size of a spaniel, look like a spaniel in their build and are coloured very similarly to spaniels. However, they are not spaniels at all and were brought about by crossing various French hounds with Spanish Pointers, Partridge Pointers and even our own English Setters untill we ended up with the dog we know today. They are without doubt a true hunt, point and retrieve breed. They have only found real favour in the UK over the last 25 years or so although British falconers were aware of them long before that. Gilbert Blaine wrote that on a hawking visit to France he had seen a very useful little dog known as a Brittany and this was way back in the 1930's

I have never owned a Brittany but I have been out with a great many and have nothing but admiration for them as a breed. I think that they, along with the Munsterlander, satisfy completely the role of an austringer's dog. Should I ever cease to fly grouse over pointers and setters then without fail I shall have a Brittany to fly my hawks over.

Spaniels

There are a number of different types of spaniel, but two are considered the norm when talking to the hawking or shooting fraternity. The English Springer and Cocker are without doubt the two types most widely used in this country. I know of one or two people that use Clumber Spaniels with their hawks but I haven't seen them in action personally. However, I have seen a couple used for shooting and I thought they were extremely slow, although very thorough, in their search for game.

Spaniels are busy energetic hunters that follow scent on the ground. The Springer gets its name from the fact that having found the game it 'springs' it into flight. The breed is medium sized with a dense coat and will penetrate the thickest of cover with boundless enthusiasm but the Cocker is a little smaller and was originally bred for finding woodcock, from which it takes its name.

Providing a spaniel works relatively close to the falconer then it can be an excellent addition to the hunting team but if they get a bit head strong and work just a little bit too far in front then many flight opportunities will be lost. A hawk flown from the fist needs a close slip when tackling game birds and accordingly the spaniel should work where the falconer wants it to, not where it wants to.

There are various other breeds which may well prove suitable for hawking but I have no personal experience of them and therefore cannot comment constructively on their suitability, or lack of it. Believe it or not, the French Poodle was originally bred for flushing ducks from the brook specifically for falconry, so I am certain that there are other breeds which could prove a useful ally to a hawk in the field. I certainly know of a Whippet cross Greyhound Lurcher that points as well as any high class pedigree dog and is hawked over regularly. Taking all things into consideration, I have come to the conclusion that the Brittany probably is as close to the perfect dog as a Harris Hawker can get. A very important consideration to be taken into account before purchasing a dog is the fact that it will be a part of your life for a considerable time, at least a decade. So, despite the fact that you should choose a dog from the breed which best meets your hawking criteria don't forget you have to look at it and be with it day in day out for years to come, so get a dog you like.

When it comes to getting a puppy make sure you get one from good working stock, preferably from a breeder you know of yourself or one that has been recommended to you. Just remember that if you buy a puppy from stock that is worth having it will not be cheap. Or, should I say it will not appear cheap initially but when you think it is going to help provide you with good sport for at least 10 years or more, as well as be a companion , then it is probably one of the cheapest investments you will ever make. There really is no such thing

Elgin pointing what turned out to be a cock pheasant.

as a cheap dog, so don't go looking for one.

The other thing to be realistic about is the future training of the dog. I am not a dog trainer, nor do I profess to be. My dogs are schooled by me and work well enough to fulfil my requirements, but I am certain a professional trainer could pick holes in them all day long. If you think that training the dog is beyond your capabilities then arrange to have it professionally trained. Again, the initial outlay involved will repay itself 10 fold, plus having a dog trained properly is nowhere near as expensive as most people seem to think it is.

As I have stated, I am not a dog trainer so I do not propose to go through the procedure of turning a bundle of limitless canine enthusiasm and energy into a sensible working companion. What you need to end up with is a dog that is obedient, works to your commands and does its job correctly. Basic training with any dog is that it must walk to heel, sit, stay and come when called. When walking to heel it must be taught to walk on the right as opposed to the more conventional left. This is for the obvious reason that the hawk is carried on the left. If you are left handed and therefore carry your hawk on the right then the dog would be taught to walk at the left heel.

You also need to ensure that you introduce hawk and dog to each other correctly and that they work in harmony. It is always easier to introduce a young hawk to a dog that is established in your household than a new dog to an older hawk that has never been around them before. But sometimes events don't always allow the introduction to be in ideal circumstances. The procedure for introducing either young or old hawks to dogs follows pretty much the same pattern but is more prolonged in the case of a puppy. When introducing a puppy to an older hawk then have the hawk on the fist and allow the puppy to run round you whilst you walk round the garden. If the hawk is allowed to pull on a decent tiring, such as the front leg of a rabbit or a pigeon wing, then so much the better. Extend these informal meetings and when the hawk is in her aviary or weathering out on the lawn allow the puppy to be in sight a great deal of the time. But, in the early days, do not allow the puppy to go too close to the hawk when she is on her bow perch. Puppies are no respecters of space or privacy and may well bound up to the hawk in play. The hawk will rather naturally resent this and will either foot the puppy or bate away from it – either way the damage to any future harmonious working relationship is done.

I have seen it recommended that you hold a puppy in your arms and let the hawk bite it on the nose. This is supposed to teach the puppy that the hawk will hurt it if it goes too close and give the hawk the feeling it is the dominant one of the two. This really is rubbish. It will just teach the puppy not to trust the hawk and probably dislike it forever and for the hawk to bite in the first place it must have been put in a situation where it felt threatened – not really the sort of start you want to a working partnership. Just allow the puppy and the hawk to gradually become used to each other naturally and without coercion. After all, if you have an eight week old puppy the days of the hawk and dog hunting together are a long way off, so there is plenty of time for them to become acquainted and relaxed with each other. Once you have got your new puppy make sure that every time you take the hawk on the fist the puppy is around. It should become almost second nature to the hawk that your presence will also include that of the dog. Even if you are going hunting and the puppy is still too young to accompany you make sure it is running around whilst you weigh the hawk and make your daily preparations. What the puppy must learn is a deep respect for the hawk without ever feeling jealous of it and this it learns at a very early age.

If your hawk is housed in an aviary or a weathering that can have a front put on then let the puppy be in sight of the hawk as much as possible. This is also a situation where a high perch can be of immense value. The high perch puts the hawk up out of the way of the young pup but means that they are still in close proximity to each other. The puppy can have its food and water bowls placed near to the base of the perch so that it repeatedly approaches the hawk from different angles. The puppy cannot possibly reach the hawk and the hawk should not feel threatened being up out of harm's way. Hawks really are very resilient creatures and do accept change quite readily providing it is of no threat to them. So, make sure that having a new puppy around does not offer any real or perceived threat to the hawk.

When the puppy is slightly older and has a degree of obedience then it can start accompanying you and the hawk in the field, even if the young dog is of no real practical use yet. The hawk can be cast off into a tree and then called back to the fist whilst the young dog is made to sit and stay a short distance away. These lessons are gradually taken forward until the hawk will fly over the dog to get back to the fist. The emphasis here is being on the word gradually. Do not rush these lessons. If things are done right you will have a partnership that will last for many years. Once the stage is reached where the hawk will happily fly over the dog to come back to the fist then the dog can be allowed to run around whilst the hawk returns to the falconer. If the hawk does this without taking any notice of the dog then you can consider that the hawk has totally accepted the dog. It would then be reasonable to hope that

A team that works in harmony together.

Esme, sister of Elgin. A truly tireless Setter that never ever seems to run out of energy and the will to work.

when you graduate to hunting as a team all should go smoothly.

When hunting does commence the hawk will very soon pick up on the fact that it is the dog that is supplying game for it to chase. I have an old female Harris Hawk that has worked with my dogs for the last 13 seasons and when she sees a dog come on point I can feel her tensing herself ready for the push off of the fist. Years ago I had access to a huge wood that was well populated with rabbits. I was then flying a male Harris and it spent a great deal of its time following on, but it was clear to see that it would follow the dog in preference to any falconer. When it saw the dog come on point it would immediately fly to the nearest available tree and peer down at the dog. Nobody ever taught it to do this, the reaction to the point came about because the hawk had sufficient intelligence to realise that it was the dog that was producing quarry for him to chase.

When the hawk has made a kill I always call my dogs over and have them lay down close to myself and the hawk. I want them to see their efforts were worthwhile, and also they get a great deal of praise for finding the game. I really do enjoy seeing hawks and dogs working together and I like to think my dogs relish the work they do. But be careful that they don't come so close as to crowd the hawk and make her feel intimidated.

I have seen a hawk that happily worked with dogs for five seasons ruined in this respect

Head study of a German Short Haired Pointer, without doubt one of the most popular breeds of working dog amongst those that fly hawks.

in a matter of a single afternoon. A falconer I knew ran a German Short Haired Pointer when hunting with his hawk but the dog had injured its leg quite badly at the start of the hawking season. Someone he knew also had a GSP and offered to run it for him so he could get some decent hawking in. All was fine until the hawk caught a rabbit and the dog attempted to take it off of her. Despite the instant shout from the owner of the dog the GSP tried for a few more seconds to wrestle the rabbit away from the hawk, then the hawk flew off in disgust and now will not tolerate being in the field with a dog – even the one she had worked with so harmoniously for five years.

Many authors make a great deal of the fact that in general Harris Hawks do not like dogs. Some say that this tendency is because the only enemy the Harris has in the wild is the Coyote. This is absolute rubbish as the hawk has many natural enemies including a of couple of surprising ones. In Mexico I saw a female Harris Hawk chase and capture a rabbit. The rabbits in Mexico are scrawny little things about half the size of a decent rabbit here. Whilst engrossed in killing the rabbit several Caracaras gathered and then attacked the Hawk on the ground. If you look at a Caracara and then at a Harris Hawk you would assume that the Hawk would deal with the scavenger with ease and would be under no real threat, but the family group of Caracaras soon killed and ate the hawk. The very fact that the Harris Hawk was

German Short Haired Pointer locked on point.

hunting on her own may well have indicated that she was not up to full strength.

I have also witnessed another Harris Hawk in the wild being killed by a female Red Tailed Hawk. The Harris Hawk was hunting with three other family members around a large pond on a vast cattle ranch in central Mexico. The pond was surrounded by bushes and small trees and was the only vegetation of any note for miles around. As the Hawks worked their way through the cover, presumably looking for rodents, the Red Tail came out of nowhere and snatched one of the hawks that had drifted slightly apart from the rest. The Red Tail stooped in just like a falcon and I can only assume it had been on the soar and took the opportunity when it presented itself. The other three Harris Hawks took absolutely no notice and carried on with their foraging.

The Coyote is not liked by Harris Hawks because it too is a highly adaptable scavenger and will take any opportunity for a meal it can. Therefore, if a Coyote pack member sees a group of hawks suddenly go down to the ground it realises they have probably made a kill and will go and investigate the possibility of stealing an easy meal. Just the same way in which a family group of Harris Hawks will congregate if they witness a Red Tail or a Ferruginous making a kill.

Harris Hawks, as with most hawks, tend not to like dogs because they think of them as fellow predators and one that could well do them harm. They tend to express themselves vocally about the situation more than other raptors because they are truly social hawks. It is in their nature to communicate their feelings freely. A Goshawk or Red Tailed Hawk will dislike dogs with an equal intensity but will express itself by bating wildly as opposed to shouting. It is the job of the falconer to convince the hawk that this is not the case and in this instance that quite the reverse is true. By accepting and then working with the dog the hawk will benefit

Hungarian Vizla. A breed that is finding quite a strong following with falconers, particularly those that fly larger hawks.

A Springer Spaniel. Exceedingly useful for finding and flushing game from close cover. Tireless and seemingly oblivious to thorns and plants that sting. Just don't know when to stop working.

Cocker Spaniel from working lines. Lovely little dogs that fulfil the same role as the Springer.

greatly from the relationship.

I like to use a transmitter collar on my dogs when out hunting, it gives a signal just like the transmitter we put on a hawk except that the regularity of the bleeps it emits will vary depending on whether the dog is running or standing on point. This can be very useful when you are working thick cover or are in a dense wood. I purchased the transmitter collars originally to use with my dogs when they are working the grouse moors. This is because they are then required to cover great tracts of ground and are often out of sight over a ridge or perhaps down in a peat hag. Either way the telemetry set will pick up their signal and tell me if they are running or if they are on point. Now they have become just as much of a habit for me to use as putting a transmitter on the hawk and I have found them extremely useful even in low ground hawking situations. Imagine your dog has worked some relatively heavy cover and you know she is nearby but can't actually pin point her. If you constantly call or whistle you stand a good chance of disturbing the game she is pointing. The same thing will happen if you go into the cover looking for her. But because of the transmitter collar you can accurately locate her and then set yourself and the hawk up accordingly for the ensuing flight.

Many years ago, before transmitter collars, I was out hunting with my female Harris Hawk and my pointer. We were working some ground I had not been on before and it was a mix of grass fields and quite heavy reed beds. I lost sight of my dog and blew the whistle to call her back in but she did not appear. I called and called for 10 minutes or so but still no dog. I was starting to worry that something serious had happened to her but as it turned out she was on point on a pheasant in the middle of the reeds and would not come off point, as is the case of course with many pointers. I prematurely flushed the pheasant by crashing around looking for her. Had I been able quickly to locate her, as I am capable of doing now, I wouldn't have lost the pheasant flight and wouldn't have had to endure 10 minutes of worry that my dog had hurt itself.

These telemetry collars are not to be confused with the training collars that are capable of being used to give the dog wearing it an electric shock whensoever the owner or trainer desires. I have absolutely no time whatsoever for them and have never ever used one and certainly never will in the future. I am not, as I stated earlier, a dog trainer. I am a falconer that needs trained dogs to assist him with getting the maximum from his sport. Therefore, I try my best to use logic and kindness to guide my dogs into doing what I want them to do. Because I always have dogs from recognised working stock the job is half done for me already. Instinct takes over as the dog grows up and I just help steer its built-in behaviour patterns so that it benefits my hawking. But, I have always managed to do so without giving my dogs the shock treatment.

There is no question that ferrets are also essential for those wanting to obtain flights at rabbits, particularly in the winter when there is not so much cover about and rabbits don't tend to sit out quite so much. Obtain your ferrets from good working stock and handle them as much as possible to ensure that they are truly tame and not prone to biting the hand that quite literally feeds them. Also, remember their eyesight is quite poor and that movements of the hand should be slow and deliberate when close to them. The last thing the falconer needs is to have a ferret that is nervous of an approaching hand. It will mean that when working it will be difficult to pick up when it half emerges from a hole. The ferret will have a tendency to duck back down the hole as it becomes aware a hand is approaching. This will then lead to the ferret having to become grabbed quickly to get it back and the whole situation becomes compounded. After a short while the ferret will be useless for working as it will be a battle of wills or strategy to get it back each time it is used.

Should for any reason a ferret bites you and 'locks on', the quickest and simplest method of getting it to release is to pinch its nose so that it has to let go to be able to breathe properly.

White ferrets are supposedly to be preferred when working with hawks. The reason for this is that a polecat ferret could be mistaken by the hawk for a stoat and could well lead to the demise of ferret. I have never found this the case and I credit most hawks with more intelligence than that. Hawks react to movement but they can distinguish between a rabbit and a ferret in an instant.

What is important in the early days of working the ferrets with the hawk is that the hawk is

German Wire Haired Pointer pointing a rabbit on the edge of a moor. This lovely bitch belongs to Diana Durman-Walters, the well respected falconer and GWP breeder.

slipped only from the fist. If it is the ferret that emerges from the hole and not a rabbit then the hawk can be held back if she bates at it. It is amazing just how quickly hawks come to realise that the ferret is an ally and take virtually no notice of them at all. Also, it helps if the ferret hutch is positioned so that the hawk can see them when she is in her aviary or weathering.

When ferreting for rabbits there are a few basic rules that need to be followed. Most of which will seem blatantly obvious but are perhaps still worth mentioning. On initial inspection of a warren, to see if it is worth putting a ferret down, you must ensure that noise and above ground movement are kept to a minimum. If there are cobwebs across the entrances then, obviously, it will be a waste of time to proceed. If, however, the earth in the entrances is turned over and there are plenty of tell tale 'currants', or droppings, then it will be worth putting the ferret down. Once the ferret is down stand back and ensure you are out of direct sight of any of the holes. Standing slightly upwind is the preferred position because rabbits normally stop just short of the entrance and peer out before making a break. If they see you or another in your party they will probably opt to go back down and try and lose the ferret under ground.

Whilst waiting for a rabbit to bolt, keep still and again keep noise to a minimum. The falconer will also need to be aware of what is around the warren. Try and work out in advance which way a rabbit is likely to bolt and position yourself accordingly. Also, ensure that no one casts their shadow across a hole, this will have the same effect as letting the rabbit see you – it will probably turn back. Have patience, it can sometimes take what seems an awfully long time for the ferret to actually get the rabbit to bolt.

Do not use ferrets in the spring as the rabbits will have young under ground and these are practically defenceless against a ferret. If the ferret kills below ground it may well lie up. This simply means it will eat some of the rabbit and then have a sleep whilst you wait patiently above ground for it to re-emerge. Most people who use ferrets make sure that they are not hungry at the time of being introduced to a warren. There is no need for the ferret to be exceedingly hungry in order for it to work a warren. Just the same as it is an old wives

A Ferret. An essential companion for the serious rabbit hawker.

tale to feed a ferret on bread and milk in an attempt to stop it ever killing and eating a rabbit. Ferrets should be fed a healthy natural diet and not be desperate to get something to eat when they are taken out to work.

When ferreting there will be some additional equipment that will have to be taken into the field. A spade for digging the ferret out if need be, a small garden trowel is also a very useful item should you have to dig down. Once you know you are getting close to the ferret you don't want to be plunging the broad blade of a spade into the ground and possibly injuring the ferret. Also a ferret locator set, which is a small receiver box and transmitter collar, will be required. Just as you would not consider flying your hawk without a telemetry transmitter fitted, don't put a ferret down holes without having fitted a locator collar first. They are relatively inexpensive and surprisingly accurate so finding a ferret below ground without them would be practically impossible. Where on earth would you start your search? But with the locator collar you can dig straight to them.

chapter five
choice of hawk

In Great Britain the choice of Harris Hawk that is available to the falconer is a fairly straight forward one. Male or female, social or food imprint, crêche reared or parent reared. The decision as to which of the sexes to fly will be largely influenced by what land is available to the falconer in question and what quarry is abundant and able to be hawked there. Females are capable of taking and holding most of the quarry species that can be flown in the United Kingdom ranging from rabbit and pheasant through to, in a small number of cases, brown hares. I am referring here to flying individual hawks, not a cast or group. Males will take a very similar range of quarry although brown hares are well beyond their capabilities. There are always exceptions to every rule, but generally speaking a brown hare is just too strong and powerful for a male Harris Hawk to hold. A great many females will get kicked off hares quite easily so it is foolish to even attempt to try and encourage a male to take on such a large prey. I have caught plenty of blue hares with a male Harris but he would never even attempt to fly a brown one. For some reason blue hares just don't seem to have the fight in them that the brown ones do and most hawks find them relatively easy to subdue once they have actually caught them.

The smaller male would appear to have a very slight edge over the larger female on initial acceleration and, to some degree, agility. This agility is such that I have had an experienced male close his wings and pass between two bars of a five bar gate when in hot pursuit of a cock pheasant. Accordingly they are ideally suited for taking corvids and gulls if reasonably close slips can be obtained. They also make excellent magpie hawks providing they can be flown at them regularly and again that slips are relatively close. The sort of cover that would put an end to the flight if a falcon were being used makes no difference whatsoever to the male Harris. If the magpie takes to the refuge of a bush, hedge or small tree the hawk will simply crash in after it. Male Harris Hawks tend to be rather underrated and are nearly always over-shadowed by the larger and more powerful females. To some people they are considered second best and only to be flown if a female can't be had. Personally, I think this is a mistake and that flying males are very good fun. Over the years I really have come to enjoy flying male Harris Hawks and have taken a very wide variety of quarry with them.

It would appear that the vast majority of those that wish to fly a Harris Hawk opt for the more powerful female. The thinking would appear to be that by going for the larger female all options are then open to the falconer with regard to quarry species. This line of thought makes sense and there can be no doubt that although both male and female Harris Hawks

A young male Harris Hawk in its juvenile plumage.

will take rabbits it is far less of a struggle for a female to subdue the quarry than a male. The same is true of cock pheasants of course. Once the decision has been taken as to what sex of Harris Hawk the falconer intends to go for, the next thing that must be decided upon is how the young hawk would have been raised.

I have absolutely no time for imprints, either of the social or food variety. Harris Hawks breed so easily as natural pairs that a social imprint would not seem an overly sensible path to follow as far as future breeding requirements are concerned. I can fully understand the need for those that wish to breed Goshawks to socially imprint them. With a species that is so prone to killing its own kind I can see why it would make sense not to have to put individuals at extreme risk by putting them together. Imprinting Sparrowhawks also has logic behind it and makes sense in the case of such a small and nervous accipiter. But I really do fail to understand why someone would want to do the same to a Harris Hawk.

My own intolerance of imprint hawks, and I am fully aware that I am probably in the minority here, is that I dislike the thought of so confusing a hawk mentally that it really doesn't know what it actually is anymore. On the one hand it wants human company but is not a human. On the other it normally hates other hawks of its own kind to the point of wanting to kill them. It is one very mentally messed up creature which is neither one thing nor another. Apart from any other considerations is man right to so mess up its mind?

A particularly fine example of a young male Harris Hawk.

Some would argue that an imprint is brave and will tackle almost anything as it knows no fear. But then surely this is precisely one of the characteristics of the wild Harris Hawk's character that makes it so popular with falconers throughout the world. Most Harris Hawks in the trained state are, to all intents and purposes, fearless and will tackle more or less anything until they learn by experience what is either beyond them or simply not worth the effort. They don't have to be fooled into tackling large prey. I have had a parent reared eyass male in his first season repeatedly cuff a Roe doe about the head. Quite what he thought was going to happen I have no idea and I tended to think this was a one off example of inexperienced juvenile behaviour. But I have twice more seen Harris Hawks strike Roe Deer and on both occasions it was by very experienced adult females. I just think that hawks instinctively re-act to movement and then press ahead with an attack if they think they stand the remotest chance of succeeding. The species is, after all, a highly developed opportunist feeder and happily takes such a wide variety of quarry that it will confidently indulge in a little speculation hunting when the chance presents itself.

A mal or food imprint is just a horror to own, fly, feed or have anything at all to do

A young female on a kill in the very early stages of her career. Accordingly, the falconer has refitted her mews jesses, leash and swivel and is allowing the hawk to take its pleasure on the kill. Encouragement like this is vital in the early days of hunting together and on each kill the hawk should be thoroughly rewarded.

with. It permanently craves food and will scream incessantly for attention. Mal imprints are very easy to spot even if you happen to see one on one of the rare occasions it has its mouth closed. Its plumage, especially around its chest area, will be greasy and dishevelled and tips of primaries and tail feathers will normally be missing. This will be from the constant mantling and sitting back on its own tail. Again I feel dreadfully sorry for any hawk that ends up as a mal imprint. Mentally it is in limbo and has a life with a very narrow outlook ahead of it. Its focus morning noon and night will be food. Because its manners are generally so bad, mal imprints quite often end up getting passed from pillar to post and because they are almost valueless, they can often end up with those that have the least experience when it comes to looking after them properly.

A crêche reared Harris Hawk is normally well behaved, tolerant of man from the start of its training, and will breed naturally with others of its kind later in life. I have had a couple of crêche reared males and found them a delight to fly. One was so bold and forward in all that he did that he actually caught a small bird and brought it back to my fist to eat it just six days after he was taken up for training. But it has to be said that he was an exceptionally intelligent hawk and very adept at working out just what was best for him. His working relationship with the Pointer I was running at the time was a pleasure to watch. The hawk would watch every move that the dog made and when she came on point the hawk knew exactly what was going on. If he was on my fist at the time then he would immediately tense himself up ready to launch at whatever was in front of the dog's nose. If he was following on then he would fly to the nearest vantage point to the dog. I never had to call him over; he knew precisely what the dog locking on point could mean to him.

The only problem I have found with crêche reared hawks is that they tend to be somewhat noisy in their first season. All young Harris Hawks are vocal, especially for the first few months of their lives. But then they are sociable hawks by nature and when they are young they are looking to build a bond with the falconer. In the second season the vocalisation tends to decrease greatly and drops to a completely acceptable level. In the case of the parent reared Harris this will be practically zero but the crêche reared hawk will still communicate freely but nowhere near as loudly or persistently.

The vast majority of young domestically produced Harris Hawks that are offered for sale each year are naturally incubated and then parent reared. As to when they should be taken from their parents and how they should be treated immediately afterwards can offer opinions that differ quite considerably. Here I can only say what has worked well for me and by doing so I do not want to imply that the method or methods used by anybody else that differs from mine are wrong. It is just that, as with most things in life, we tend to stick with what works well for us. I like to leave the clutch of youngsters with their parents for 12 weeks, then the whole clutch is removed and put into a separate seclusion aviary by themselves. They are then fed for a further two to four weeks without seeing a human being and therefore associating them with food. I believe the risk of removing them from their parents and then immediately replacing the parents with a human being as a food source can lead to problems later on.

Because Harris Hawks are such sociable creatures they take longer than most hawks to mature mentally and will imprint even when several months old. Therefore I believe that taking the extra care and time to prevent any inclination to imprint is well worth the trouble. The tendency that people have to want to obtain their hawk and then get it trained and hunting as quickly as possible is a completely understandable one. But although perhaps hard to do, it is far better to take the long term approach and make sure that all the ground work towards a future harmonious relationship with the hawk is done properly. Providing your hawk does not succumb to illness or an accident, you will have the pleasure of hunting in its company for anything up to 20 years or more. So, taking a few extra weeks in the first year to ensure that the hawk is raised properly and really is a pleasure to be with in the future has got to be worthwhile. When it comes to hawks that have been produced domestically then my first option would be a parent reared example followed closely by a crêche reared one.

In many countries where the Harris Hawk is found in the wild it is still possible to take a hawk under licence for the purpose of falconry. This therefore opens up several more options to falconers as to when and how to take a new hawk. An eyass from the nest is straight forward enough and care will have to be taken not to imprint it. Branchers are also an option. These are young hawks that are out of the nest and scrabbling about the vicinity of it but are not yet

A young wild-taken female Harris Hawk in Peru.

ready to fly or indeed are capable of it. But for the ultimate Harris Hawk, at least as far as I am concerned, then it has to be the equivalent of a passage hawk. Harris Hawks don't migrate and therefore if you set about trapping a juvenile youngster you are not going to be taking it whilst it is on passage. But you will be able to get a young hawk that has learnt enough to survive for almost the first full cycle of the seasons. This is without doubt the most critical time in the life of any wild hawk and the vast majority of youngsters in their first year do not get past the age of approximately six months. But youngsters that have been fending for themselves for almost a season are still referred to as passage hawks. Those that wish to fly them normally trap them when they are nine to 10 months old and the family group may well be starting to push them away anyway.

A statement concerning wild Harris Hawks, which is repeated on a fairly regular basis, is that a family group stays together and the survivors from each clutch produced by the alpha female stay with and swell the ranks of that particular family. This is obviously not true in its literal sense. If it were then family groups would probably consist of upwards of 30 members at any one time. In actual fact Harris Hawks drive off the majority of their youngsters just as any other raptor species tends to do. It is just that they do it at a much later stage in the development of the youngsters. Some offspring will be tolerated and allowed to stay with the group if food is plentiful. But even so they are normally driven off when the dominant couple want to breed again. There are no real hard and fast rules as to family composition. I have observed many Harris Hawk families in the wild and they range from couples to seven or eight members. I have seen one family group of 16 and was fortunate enough to follow them for several days before that particular trip came to an end. But I believe this was an exceptionally large family group and I certainly have never seen another quite so large. The usual would appear to be five to seven, but for every family group you see in the wild you will also see just a pair of adult hawks together. This is particularly true of areas where food is scarce.

The qualities and merits of training and flying a passage hawk are such that, in my opinion, they put all other hawks of their species in the shade. From the falconer's point of view you have a hawk that has not had any form of close contact with man before but is very experienced in hunting. It knows how to use the wind to its advantage and also is fully aware of what it can and cannot take in terms of quarry. It will have spent a certain amount of time hunting with others of its own kind and will therefore be tolerant of them if required later in life to fly in a cast or group. But it is the hard learnt field craft that gives the passage hawk such superiority over either the wild or domestically produced eyass. Without doubt an eyass that is flown hard and at a wide variety of quarry will eventually attain the same level of knowledge and guile as a passage hawk. It is just that it will take it several seasons to do so.

Those that make statements to the effect that there is no difference between a wild and domestically produced hawk are probably correct in the case of the eyass hawk. But when comparing a passage hawk with an eyass of any description then the former is always going to have a very distinct edge. Manning a passager is quite straight forward although it will take a little longer than with an eyass. In the first few days they are highly suspicious and very wary of any movement on the part of the falconer. All actions must be exaggeratedly slow and deliberate and great care must be taken not to frighten the hawk. One careless moment could possibly ruin the relationship between hawk and falconer before it has properly begun. Making the passage hawk to the hood could not be easier provided the process is undertaken from day one of training. The hawk will still be far more wary of the falconer than any object and so hooding should be exceedingly simple.

The only real difficulty I encountered with the passage Harris Hawks that I personally have had experience with, is that they took a very long time to adapt to working with a dog. Even though time and extremely careful introduction meant that a working relationship between hawk and dog was eventually possible, it was never ever a relaxed one on the part of the hawk. In fact I remember one passage female a friend had in Mexico that just would not tolerate any dogs at all within close range of her. If we came across any dogs whilst out hawking she would make for the top of the nearest vantage point and stay there until the dog had gone.

All this talk of passage hawks may seem superfluous to a reader other than in Central or South America. But for those that wish to give the passage hawk a try and personal circumstances allow for them to concentrate on nothing else for three or four months then the opportunities are out there. Unrealistic for the majority I know, but for those with an appropriate life style that lends itself to giving such a falconry adventure a go it really is worth a try. I can assure you of this from personal experience.

chapter six
hooding

S ome of the more modern works on falconry suggest that the Harris Hawk need not be made to the hood. The reasons given for this are not normally very clear and my personal opinion is that those that offer this sort of advice do so because perhaps their own personal skills in hooding are somewhat lacking. As a matter of course all hawks should be made to hood and the benefits of doing so are blatantly clear to all, or at least they should be.

The main argument against hooding put forward by some are that a well manned hawk should never have need of the hood and the more she sees going on around her, the calmer the hawk will be. I agree completely that a hawk should be thoroughly manned and that she should be able to take most things in her stride. But there will be occasions when to be able to quickly pop a hood on the hawk will prove invaluable.

I have always been a very firm believer that a hawk is not thoroughly trained unless she has been made properly to the hood and will take it without a fuss or a struggle. The process of hooding should be calm, straightforward and stress free – at least stress free for the hawk anyway. If a hawk is made to the hood properly there is no need to constantly make her wear it. Other than if needed it can just be popped on briefly each day she is handled just to keep her familiar with it. For example, when she is taken up to be weighed would be a good time.

The advantages of being able to hood a hawk so thoroughly outweigh any conceivable argument against doing so that I fail to see why anyone wouldn't. If you are training your hawk and a stray dog or a group of inquisitive children suddenly come running up, a fraught situation for the hawk can be avoided by deft use of the hood. If the hawk sustains an injury in the field and you need to get her to a vet as quickly and as quietly as possible then again the hood will be your salvation. So much easier to take complete control of the situation when she is hooded.

Then, of course, there is the fact that you can avoid unnecessary bating on the part of the hawk when there are flights you don't want her to take on. If she can't see what you don't want her to chase then she won't waste energy and frustrate herself by bating hopelessly. This is particularly true if you are out hunting with others and it is not your turn to slip. Why tease your hawk by letting her see opportunities you have no intention of letting her take up.

Another reason to have your hawk hooded in exactly this sort of situation is it dramatically reduces the risk of another hawk which has just been slipped and has failed to kill, coming back and trying to take your hawk off of the fist. It is movement that triggers a

A superb shot of an adult female in flight.

My ten year old male Harris Hawk, Hugo, in an anglo-indian hood.

reaction in hawks as we all know. A hooded hawk sits still and is not constantly restless or bating off the fist, therefore other hawks in the party take virtually no notice of her.

Travelling to and from your training or hunting ground is another time when a hood can be useful. Nowadays, practically everyone makes full use of travelling boxes as opposed to just having a hawk tied to a cadge or portable perch in the back of the car. Most hawks take to travelling boxes very well indeed and go in and out without problems and sit quiet for the duration of the journey. But there are some that don't like going in boxes and are extremely restless once inside them. These two problems are immediately eradicated with the use of the hood.

The choice of hood is realistically limited to three basic styles or variants of them. The traditional Dutch, with its more modern American counterpart, the Bahraini and the Anglo Indian. All modern hoods, no matter what their style, are now so much lighter than the hoods of 15 or 20 years ago. Then no one would have used a Dutch hood on a hawk as they were heavy and the slot style beak opening was far from suitable. In fact use of this type of hood my well have actually made the hawk hood shy, purely and simply because the hood was heavy

Hugo again, this time in a dutch hood.

and uncomfortable, especially round the sensitive skin of the mandible. American style Dutch hoods are so much lighter and have a totally redesigned beak opening that is comfortable for the hawk.

Bahraini hoods are nice and simple to use and actually are probably the easiest of all the styles to slip on to a hawk, especially one in the early stages of hooding. The shape of the hood lends itself well to dropping down into place on the head of the hawk. Bahraini hoods are normally unblocked, although some hood makers do now block them, and are therefore generally soft and pliable. They are also quite forgiving when you have scrunched them up in your pocket when out in the field. They reform their shape very readily.

Anglo Indian hoods are probably the most widely used and these can be either blocked or unblocked. If a blocked Anglo Indian is a good fit then there is very little to compare to it when it comes to satisfying the criteria the falconer should be looking for. That is that the hawk cannot see out of it, that she cannot hook it off with a deft movement of her foot, she can cast through it if need be and it does not touch any part of her mandible or the skin around it. An unblocked hood will be a little more forgiving in this last respect but an ill-fitting blocked hood will irritate and cause the hawk distress as well as teach her to learn to hate the hood.

I have not mentioned that the beak opening of the hood should be sufficient to allow the hawk to feed through it as well as cast. This is for the simple reason that I never ever feed a hawk through the hood. I think it is a dreadful habit to teach a hawk and one that will cause irritation to the falconer for the rest of their working relationship, which could be a very long time. A hawk that has been fed through the hood will constantly pick at the glove when she is being carried hooded. She will expect carriage and hooding together to mean food is on hand and will look for it.

It may well seem a ridiculous thing and a blatantly obvious one to say but the hood should fit well. But you would be amazed at just how many hawks are not equipped with hoods that do the job they were designed to do properly. Mavrogordato used to state that a good test of how well a hood fitted was for the falconer to have the hooded hawk on his fist and then take hold of the plume and gently pull it down towards the hawks' feet. The amount of so called perfectly fitting hoods that pop off when you do so would certainly surprise you. But then so would the number of hooded hawks that can actually see out of their hoods. This is certainly not desirable as the hawk could well strike at any glimmer of movement it can partially see.

The other thing to be avoided at all costs is the hood constantly touching the skin. As well as causing untold irritation this can also cause infection. I have seen several cases of hawks that have been quite ill because the places the hood rubs are constantly being opened up and thereby re-infected each time the hood is used.

For someone who has not hooded a hawk before but wishes to do so I would suggest using either a Bahraini or an Anglo Indian. Both are slightly easier than the Dutch to put on and also to get a perfect fit. It is easy enough to alter slightly the fit of the beak opening on the Bahraini and Anglo Indian by lightly wetting the leather either side of the opening and rolling it back slightly with your fingers, this will open it up just a little. If the corners of the opening touch the beak or skin around it then gently trimming the hood with a scalpel will ease this problem. But trim carefully and err on the side of taking off too little, you can always take a little more off but you can never put any material back. If you cut back too far then the hood is ruined.

The fit around the neck of an Anglo Indian can also be adjusted although most people don't realise it. The lash that is interwoven around the base of these hoods is not there for decorative purposes, it is there as an adjustment. It can be tightened or slackened off as required. The adjustment is only a slight one but it can well make the difference between a perfectly fitting hood and one that can be removed by the hawk.

A hood that does not fit properly is of no use whatsoever and no falconer would be able to relax knowing that a hawk he has left hooded may well be able to get the hood off if she really tries hard. This being never truer than if she has been left in the proximity of other hawks. If she does manage to get her hood off another hawk may well pay with its life for the fact that a hood that fitted correctly wasn't used. So it pays to take time and care when selecting a hood and ensuring you get exactly what you are after. If you make your own hoods and end up with one that fits all your requirements then my advice would be to immediately make another one as a spare. If you purchase your hoods from equipment suppliers and get exactly what you are after then invest in a spare. It will pay dividends.

Whether you make your own hoods or purchase them from furniture suppliers a very important point is to ensure that the hoods are fitted with Gortex braces. Leather braces are almost a thing of the past, or at least they should be. When they get damp they bind and the hood becomes practically impossible to undo. I have known occasions, such as being caught out in a torrential rain storm, when the braces of a hood have had to be cut to get the hood off of the hawk. When the weather is very hot they give slightly and the back of the hood can spring slightly apart. This effectively means the hood becomes partially undone, the braces themselves wear relatively quickly and have to be replaced on a regular basis. With Gortex material none of these problems occur, even when wet the braces will operate as they should and they practically never wear out.

Making a fresh hawk to the hood is a fairly straight forward process and should hold no fears even for the novice falconer. The key to getting the whole thing right is confidence. The more you hesitate when trying to hood a hawk in the early stages, then the harder and harder it will become. You will transmit your nervousness to the hawk and she will try with all her might to avoid your tentative attempts at placing the hood on her head. She will show you her wonderful impression of a snake and weave her head from side to side and frustrate your efforts to hood her.

I always introduce a hawk to the hood at the earliest stages of training. Endeavour to make the hawk to the hood whilst she is still more wary of you than she is anything else. Some falconers, especially beginners, make the mistake of leaving the introduction of the hood until the hawk is steady on the fist and will eat there without any hesitation. This is a definite mistake as now she has accepted you and will concentrate her efforts on the hood. Also, she will associate you with something that is not altogether pleasant. Whereas if you hood her literally from day one then she will accept the hood as she gradually learns to accept you.

The first few hooding lessons should be carried out when you are in the right frame of mind to do them. This may seem an odd thing to say but it is no good trying something that may well lead to a frustrating time if you are not perfectly calm and relaxed yourself. If things do not go as planned and the hawk flicks the hood off for the 20th time it is of no use getting in a temper and cursing and swearing. It won't do any good whatsoever and it will be a positively bad lesson for the hawk. She will associate the hood with a scene and this will make her nervous and even less responsive to any future lessons. No matter how frustrating the initial lessons the falconer must stay calm at all times and do nothing that will cause the hawk to become flustered. It has to be said that I'm not exactly renowned for being the calmest and most laid back person and, accordingly, I pick my moments to introduce a new hawk to the hood very carefully.

When you decide to hood your hawk for the first time get yourself nice and comfortable and resign yourself to the fact that it is probably going to be a frustrating time. If you do it in the very early stages of training, as I do myself, then the hawk is still at the stage where it sits on the fist with wings open, mouth slightly ajar and will bate readily at the slightest thing. There will be food on the fist that she may or may not be contemplating eating.

It is important that you put yourself and the hawk in the correct position for hooding. You want to make the whole operation go as smoothly as possible and it is attention to detail that

Hugo once more, but this time wearing a Bahraini or Arab hood.

is the key to success. When your hawk is nicely settled on the fist bring your left arm so that it is across your body and the hawk is directly facing you with her head at about the height of your chin. Her head will ideally be about nine inches or so from your face and this will mean that once the hood is in place it will be a simple matter to lean forward and take one set of braces in your teeth, the other set in your right hand and then close the hood. As you go to close the hood lower your own head slightly so that you are pulling the braces away from the body of the hood and in a slightly downward manner. This will often prevent the hawk from flicking it off just before you have closed the hood and will also ensure the hood sits back fully on the neck of the hawk.

But we are running before we can walk. First of all we actually need to get the hood on the hawk. The simplest and normally most effective way is as follows:- Take the hood by the top knot and hold it towards her chest upside down and with the front of the hood nearest to her. Raise your hand so that the hood is high enough that the tip of her beak is almost in the body of the hood and then roll your hand up and over so that the hood goes over the head and drops down in place in one deft movement. If luck is on your side then she may well ponder for a few seconds what on earth has happened to her. If you are fortunate enough for this to occur then try and get the hood done up. But what is far more likely to follow is that she will either bate and dislodge the hood or simply flick her head and you will have to retrieve the hood from the floor.

The important thing is not to be discouraged but to calmly proceed. Just repeat the process until eventually you succeed in having the hood in place and the braces are tightened. The reaction, on the part of the hawk, is to pretend she has suddenly been paralysed and she will fall from the fist and hang upside down stiff legged. As you attempt to lift her back onto the fist her feet will initially refuse to grip and she will fall from the fist again. This normally passes pretty quickly and then what follows is that we have to endure the "kill the fist moment" followed by "must get this thing off at all costs" moment. The footing of the glove does not last long but the shaking the head and trying to hook the hood off may continue for several moments. The best way to help this end quickly is to walk with the hawk once she has been successfully hooded. Whereas, previously, you have taken great care to make the carriage of the hawk as smooth and as gentle as possible now a little unsteadiness in the carriage is a positive help. The hawk will have to concentrate on her grip and therefore will not be able to expend quite so much energy on removing the hood.

Do not leave the hood on for too long on the first few occasions. Try and get the hawk hooded more than once in each session. Also don't wait until the end of the meal, if she will eat on the fist at this stage, as you don't want the hawk to associate the hood with a negative thing. The ending of the meal would certainly be a negative thing to a hawk that is having reduced rations. When progress is being made try popping the hood on, leaving it in place for a few seconds, and then taking it off again without doing up the braces. Repeat the process but this time do the braces up. Try not to fall into a routine at this stage and form any regular routine relating to the hood and its use.

There is a little trick which may prove useful if you have a hawk that gets the hood off before you get a chance to do the braces up. As soon as the hood is in place slide your fingers from the plume down to the braces. Take the long brace of the right hand side of the hood as you look at it between your index finger and thumb. Whilst your forefinger presses gently against the body of the hood, where the braces are attached, pull the brace with your fingers. The result of this is that the hood will effectively half close. This will make it very difficult for the hawk to flick it off. When she has had a few moments to settle you can then lean forward and take both sets of braces in fingers and teeth, in the orthodox method, and finish closing the hood properly.

In no time at all, providing you have not been heavy handed, the hawk will happily wear the hood and you should be able to put it on her without any fuss or struggle. At this early stage of her training you should make the effort to hood her often and really reinforce that training. The old expression that covered this stage of the hawk's training was breaking to the hood. It is a term I really don't like as it suggests a roughness and possible coercion. I far prefer the term making to the hood. Hal Webster has often said that in his view hawks and falcons are guided to do what the falconer requires of them rather than be trained. To a certain extent I would agree with this in that the education of the hawk or falcon should be a series of positive steps forward that have been brought about by the falconer understanding the point of view of the hawk and anticipating its requirements and reactions.

When it comes to unhooding the hawk be just as calm and relaxed as if hooding her. Position the hawk correctly and then strike the braces on the hood. Do not then whip it off. Leave the hood struck for a few seconds and then remove it. If you quickly whip it off each time the braces are struck the hawk will learn to anticipate the moment and when she feels you take hold of the braces she will flap her wings or worse still bate in anticipation. This is a bad lesson that is learnt very quickly if you strike the hood, whip it off and cast her at quarry. If it means missing a flight because you don't get the hood off in two seconds flat then so be it. There will be plenty more throughout your hawking association.

A hawk that has been made properly to the hood never forgets the lessons taught. I remember a female Harris Hawk I had some years back which I lent to a friend who was without a hawk at the time. When the hawk was handed over she was accompanied by her hood. After two seasons the hawk was brought back to me and it transpired that during the entire period she was away she had not been hooded once. The falconer I had lent her to wasn't confident in hooding and had decided that not using the hood on her at all was the easier option.

As soon as the hawk was back with me this became apparent as she did her best to avoid having the hood put on. But in just three days she was completely happy to wear the hood again. We just went through the early stages of training again as if it was all completely new to her. She wasn't forced into the hood but gently led into accepting it again.

Always remember to be smooth and positive in your actions when hooding your hawk. Take great care to avoid making a hawk hood shy. A lot of novices attempt to hood a hawk for the first time and because it bobs, weaves and ducks its head they state it is hood shy and give up trying. The hawk is merely trying to avoid the unknown and not have the hood fitted. A truly hood shy hawk will bate or scream at the sight of the hood and will probably never be brought round.

A great many falconry books end their chapter or section on hooding with a long and difficult to read quotation from Edmund Bert. It is difficult to read because it is in Elizabethan English and the method described of making a hawk to the hood was also specifically written for those that trained passage Goshawks. I do not recommend the method related in the book as it involves teaching the hawk to put its head in the hood by the use of food. As mentioned earlier I never ever want a hawk of mine to feed through the hood or to think there is the opportunity to feed through the hood. Edmund Bert was obviously a superbly skilful falconer and had probably forgotten more about falconry than I will ever know. But on this one point I dare to differ in my opinion.

Nevertheless, I would recommend any falconer, particularly those that train principally short and broad winged hawks, to read *An Approved Treatise of Hawkes and Hawking*. Fortunately the volume has now been edited and transcribed into modern English by Derry Argue.

Finally, I would like to relate an incident that happened in Scotland a few years back between myself and a falconer that never hoods any of his hawks. We have often had discussions about the merits of hooding hawks and he is as firmly against it as I am for it. Several friends and I were hawking rabbits, with the aid of a couple of ferrets, in some fields close to a road. It was almost the end of the season and soon the hawks would be put up to moult. The other falconer was driving past and spotted us, he parked up and walked over to join us and see how we were doing. I had a female Harris Hawk on the fist and another falconer had a male. It was the turn of the male to be slipped next and accordingly my hawk was hooded.

The new arrival made a point of shouting out that if you have to hood a Harris Hawk then it can't be properly manned and shouldn't be in the field. Although the remark was supposedly good humoured banter I knew there was an underlying antagonism beneath it. We traded sarcastic remarks for a few minutes and then I asked him if he had his hawk with him, he replied it was in the van and ready to go. He was offered the opportunity to join us and duly fetched his hawk, an intermewed male Red Tail.

A rabbit was bolted and the male Harris Hawk slipped at it. Despite a good chase and flight the rabbit made the safety of another burrow and the male Harris Hawk returned to the fist. Whilst he had been hunting the rabbit the watching Red Tail had bated repeatedly from the fist. It was then my turn to fly my female and another rabbit was eventually bolted. She flew and took her rabbit. The Red Tail bated not only whilst she was flying but also while she was being taken up from her kill, which is something I do not believe in rushing.

The result of all this bating was that one of the three remaining intact tail feathers of the Red Tail broke and a large piece floated to the ground. I remarked on this and was told that you had to expect this sort of thing with a hunting hawk towards the end of the season. I then noticed that the Red Tail had quite a few wing tips missing as well and was told that this is down to the fact he gets restless in the back of the van, where he sits on a portable bow perch, and scuffs them when he bates.

The Harris Hawk on my fist, which had been hunted hard all season long, was feather perfect. She didn't bate when other hawks were hunting and she sits quietly in her travelling box. Both of which are due not only to her being well manned but also to her being made to the hood. I rest my case.

Hawking can be a sociable affair.

chapter seven
training

Training basically falls into four clearly defined stages that should be a logical progression, one following the other smoothly and efficiently. Manning is the first. This covers getting the hawk used to man and everything associated with him, being made to the hood and feeding on the fist. The second is calling off where the hawk is encouraged, through manning and dieting, to fly ever increasing distances to the fist in response to the falconers prompt to do so. This stage would have the humble beginnings of a step to the fist. Then, jumping leash length both indoors and out, finally moving on to use of the creance which should culminate in the hawk flying free. The third is getting fit and muscled up so that the hawk has the fitness and stamina to tackle wild quarry with a reasonable chance of success. Last, but not least stage four, entering to wild quarry. This is where skill and understanding on the part of the falconer can make the hawk. Lack of them could possibly mar a hawk forever. Entering is, in my opinion, worth looking at in greater detail and therefore the chapter following this one is devoted entirely to it.

A point worth remembering is that all hawks are constantly learning and that training as such is a continual process, this is particularly so in the case of the Harris Hawk. Of all the hawks they must surely be the most intelligent and quick to learn. The fact that they are naturally sociable means that it is possible to develop a working partnership that really is based on mutual trust and respect, as opposed purely to diet. I can think of no other species where it is possible to build up such a close working relationship. With this in mind the falconer must always be wary of mistakes made in training or accidental negative enforcement. Once instilled, a bad habit is exceedingly difficult to eradicate in a Harris Hawk.

Whether we have bred the hawk we intend to fly ourselves, or it has come to us from a breeder, the first thing to do when the youngster comes out of the aviary is to get it fitted with its furniture. Hopefully, the last few days that the young hawk had spent in the aviary would have seen its food ration reduced somewhat. This would be in an effort to ensure that the hawk was not grossly overweight and stood a chance of being reasonably responsive with regard to food within the next few days. I normally take young hawks from the aviary and fit their equipment when the light of the day is starting to fail. Once equipped with their furniture, which does include a telemetry transmitter tail mount, I leave them overnight tethered to a bow perch somewhere nice and quiet. I know full well they will be restless and probably bate quite a lot therefore I often put a hood on them if I can't put them in a completely darkened room. It is also important to make sure that if they bate their wings tips are not going to brush against

Adult female Harris Hawk returning to the fist.

any surfaces which could damage them. Before putting them away for the night I would have weighed them to have a record of their starting weight.

Bright and early the next day, I take the hawk up on the fist and begin the manning process. From now on the routine I follow is a fairly straight forward one in that the hawk is taken up on the fist, hooded and then weighed at the start of each session. There are two entirely different schools of thought when it comes to the time that should be spent manning a new hawk. The first is the saturation technique where the hawk is on the fist for as much of the day as can possibly be arranged. The alternative is the approach whereby the hawk is handled for an hour or so at a time, twice a day. My own belief is that in the early days of training you can very easily handle a hawk too much. You want each step with the hawk to be one that goes forward and if you make each individual lesson with the hawk too long then she may well resent you taking her up on the fist. She is going to be wary of you anyway so there is no point in compounding her feelings and making her longing to be anywhere but on the fist.

What is absolutely essential is that all these early lessons are positive steps and not negative ones. Plan ahead before taking the hawk up on the fist and try and forestall any possible awkward moments for the hawk. For my first few lessons I like to walk to a chair in a quiet spot in the garden with a hedge behind me and a wall behind the hawk. It is a shaded spot so I don't have to worry about excess sun and it is not possible for anything to approach from behind me. As I hawk with the aid of dogs then I always ensure that at least one of the dogs is present at all the early lessons. In the morning sessions I have a decent tiring for the hawk, which it will rarely look at in the first day or two. In the evening session I then try and get the hawk to feed properly and do all I can to encourage it. Simple things like moving the food with my thumb to try and focus the attention of the hawk, breaking bits off and offering them at beak height. What is very important in these early stages is to keep touching the hawk around the feet and legs. You need to be able to change from mews to flying jesses later in the hawks career and you don't want to run the risk of being footed every time you do so. It might appear to be overly cautious, but I always make a point of showing the hawk I have no food in my hand before I try and touch its feet. The hawk can also be stroked with a feather all over its body and its feet as part of the manning process. This is particularly useful as it means that the plumage of the hawk is not being stroked by the hand of the falconer and thereby having its natural oils removed.

After several days the hawks weight will be reducing somewhat and her responses will be getting sharper towards food that is offered. It is important not to crash the weight of the hawk at all and should it prove particularly stubborn then still allow it a small amount of food each day as long as it does not appear to come from you. By that I mean if the hawk will just not feed and hasn't done so for several days then when you put her back on the bow at the end of the session have a skinned and gutted chick that you can slip beside her bow perch. Sooner or later the hawk will spot the chick and eat it. This way you are sure her system is kept working and her appetite will actually be encouraged. If you stop feeding her altogether she will shut down her system and take even longer to feed initially on the fist. Hawks are like humans if you want them to lose weight then food on a little and often basis is better than none at all.

Normally after a few days the hawk will feed on the fist without too much hesitation and now progress will be at a much more rapid rate – not that there is any rush. Once a hawk will feed readily I then introduce the whistle. I use a football referee whistle and just blow it gently each time I present food to the hawk. To give the hawk a full blast when it is already sitting on the fist would probably not endear her to it, but once she has reached the stage of being called off then I do blow the whistle properly. Obviously I am trying to create the condition where the hawk associates the blowing of the whistle with a food reward and this will help at a later stage of her career when she is flying at quarry. It will be another very effective recall mechanism.

In between the manning sessions the hawk will be placed on her bow where she can see life going on all around her. Do not starve her of mental stimulation and let her see the dog or dogs she will be working with in the future. Once she will sit relatively quietly offer her a bath each morning but take it away again after midday. Removing the bath away at this time is merely a precaution against her taking a late one and having to be put away for the night wet.

Once she is responding well to the glove and the food that is on it you can start taking her for walks and carry on with the first stages of manning. This is where the use of tirings really will pay dividends. The hawk will step up from the bow quite eagerly in anticipation of getting some food and the tiring will allow her to pull for a considerable time without actually getting any food from it. But it will serve its purpose in that it will help to keep her occupied and reduce the risk of any repetitive bating. Whilst out on these manning strolls, occasionally hood the hawk for a few moments, sometimes doing the braces of the hood up and sometimes not. Leave the hawk hooded for a moment or two and then unhood her again. The point of this is twofold: the first is to carry on making the hawk to the hood and by varying the times and places the hood has no bad associations for the hawk. As, for example, it would do if she is only ever hooded at the end of the meal. The second is that the hood can be used to avoid a scene that you feel the hawk is not yet ready to face at this early stage of her career. For example, a noisy group of children on bicycles or several riders on horses. It is also possible to start jumping the hawk to the fist from fence posts and rails whilst on these strolls. So take a few chick legs or a front leg of rabbit with you, do not call her to the fist with the tiring as a reward. Realistically there is nothing on it that is why you are using it as such, you want her to think that making the effort to jump to the fist is a worthwhile exercise and one that will hold a reward for her.

When the hawk has reached the stage where she will readily step up to the fist from the bow and can be hooded without any problems then it's time to gently move on to the next stage of her training, calling off. The last job before doing so is to introduce the hawk to the lure. It makes no difference in my opinion whether it is a bird lure or a dummy bunny. The hawk is not stupid enough to think it is real either way. This is a very simple process and the lure, with food on it, is simply dropped down in front of the hawk whilst she is sitting on her bow and the whistle is blown. Any Harris Hawk worth their salt will jump straight down onto it and eat the food that is on it. They can then be taken back up on the fist, replaced on the bow and the process repeated. Sometimes the hawk can prove difficult to pick up off the lure and clings on to it for dear life. The easiest way to deal with this situation is to make the lure disappear by covering it over with your hawking bag or a piece of cloth whilst at the same time proffering the fist with some food on it. Later when being 'called off' on the creance, the lure can be substituted for the fist occasionally to reinforce the meaning of the lure and to make the lesson a little different for the hawk. There will be times when the falconer will be glad he made his hawk to the lure. When a hawk has become spooked or has gone into a mood and is reluctant to come down to the fist, the lure will nearly always be too tempting for the hawk to resist. Once she is down in the ground she will then normally step up onto the glove quite happily.

The next stage is a simple and logical progression for the hawk and involves encouraging it to fly ever increasing distances to the falconer, normally for a food reward. As soon as the hawk will jump readily leash length from the bow then it is time to move on. Personally, I never ever call a hawk more than leash length from the bow perch as I don't want to encourage it to think it can prove worthwhile to bate from the bow. I use a high perch or T-perch in the early stages and call her on the creance. When it comes to the use of the creance there have been many stupid accidents over the years and probably all of them have been completely unnecessary. Whenever the creance is attached it should be tied to the slits in the mews jesses, not to the swivel, which would have been removed. Also, I never ever use a creance line that has a spring clip or any other form of rapid attachment mechanism. I have seen too many breakages and heard of too many hawks being lost with their legs still shackled together by the means of the swivel. Unless recovered quickly their fate will not be a pleasant one. Something I have got into the habit of doing in recent years is fitting a telemetry transmitter, even when I am carrying out training flights on the creance. This way if something does go wrong I can at least track the hawk down. Also, the hawk has to get used to having the transmitter fitted and then flying with it, so why not do so right from the word go.

When first calling a new hawk on a line the temptation is to try and make progress very quickly. Because the hawk came 10 yards on the first day don't get impatient and try to get her to come 50 yards the next. In fact, each day you should start the lessons almost aback at the beginning and just give the hawk one or two really close jumps to act as reminders and confidence boosters. Soon enough she will be coming the full length of the creance and if

A successful outcome. Maud at the age of twelve on a kill.

you are on your own you will probably be finding it difficult to get far enough away from her to be able to call her the full distance you really want to. This is where a friend can come in really useful. On no account be tempted to use a dragged creance. This is a creance line that has been taken off of the handle and the hawk can fly off with only the weight of the line to impede its progress. The use of dragged creances is again an accident waiting to happen, in my opinion. Needless to say the same applies to casting off a hawk to a tree with a creance of any description in place. It doesn't matter if the tree has plenty of bare branches that stick out just where you want them to; the hawk is bound to land on one that does have branches for it to get snagged on.

A few days will normally see creance work dispensed with and the hawk can be flown free and moved onto the next stage which is getting fit and building some muscle. Calling off requires that the hawk is recalled longer and longer distances to the fist. This can be out of trees or off fence rails. Once the hawk has come back to the fist and given a very small reward it is then cast off again to another perch. The process is repeated over and over until the hawk is either showing signs of flagging, which is extremely unlikely, or the falconer is running out of small pieces of food, known more correctly as bechins, to give the hawk as a reward.

Another way of getting the hawk fit initially is to go for long walks and have the hawk following on. The problem with this type of exercise is that the hawk is able to glide as opposed to fly for much of the time, which does not do a great deal towards building muscle. Also, most hawks out like this will spot quarry sooner or later and drop down onto or give chase, then you have unwittingly planted the seeds of self hunting.

Two other methods can be employed which will help to get the hawk fit and both are designed to build muscle quite quickly. The first is calling the hawk to the fist from the ground. The falconer places the hawk on the ground and then stands almost over it and the glove is

Dale Fairbrass assisting his adult female Harris Hawk, Anita, despatching her quarry.

raised above the head of the falconer and the hawk then called to it. Because the hawk must pump up almost vertically it really is a very strenuous exercise and the hawk develops hard muscle and good breathing capacity very quickly. This form of exercise is also excellent for when the weather is just too bad to give the hawk any work at all outdoors.

Another relatively new method is flying a hawk to a lure suspended from a kite. The technique is very popular amongst those that fly falcons and it is possible, in a remarkably short time, to get a falcon fit enough to climb up to a 1000 feet without showing any signs of fatigue. I have tried this particular method with one male Harris Hawk and it certainly got him very fit. I only got him to climb to around 200 feet as it was just an experiment and I had to return the kite to its owner. I do know of another falconer that had a female Harris that would go over 400 feet to the kite without any hesitation.

A way of making a young hawk work really hard, when exercising it, is to fly it with the wind up its tail instead of flying it directly into it. All hawks prefer to take off and land into the wind for exactly the same reason that aircraft do, that is stability and control. If you call a young hawk to the fist the wrong way it will go past you at a rate of knots and then have to turn back and struggle to reach the fist. They really have to labour to control themselves, turn round and then come back.

Once the falconer is sure the hawk is fit and ready to hunt quarry then the process of entering can begin.

chapter eight
entering

In theory, entering your hawk is as easy as falling off of a log. You take your freshly trained hawk out to suitable hunting area, allow her to chase prey until she latches on and manages to hold something and there we are, she is entered. In practical terms it does not normally work out like that. A little thought and forward planning can ease the whole process forward so that the hawk suffers very little disappointment or the chance of a set-back. The first few flights at quarry are crucial and can shape the future of your years of hunting together. It is vitally important to get the hawk a kill as soon as possible.

Accordingly, as a falconer you must be selective about the slips you offer the hawk in the initial stages of hunting. The hawk also needs to play its part as well and it is surprising just how many young hawks do not chase the first few quarry opportunities that are presented to them. It is very frustrating and hard to understand what is going on in a hawk's mind when it refuses what appears to be the simplest of chances. You have done your part by engineering a slip that should give the young hawk the advantage, only to be rewarded by having the hawk simply watch the quarry make good its escape without giving chase at all. The thing to do is not lose heart and keep on offering the hawk opportunities to make a kill. Sooner or later it will switch on and act more as you would expect a hawk to.

The very first consideration to be taken into account before trying to enter the new hawk is its fitness. The falconer must be sure that he has brought his hawk to the field with sufficient muscle to enable the hawk to stand a reasonable chance of chasing quarry. Nothing succeeds like success and it is vital for the confidence of the young hawk that it meets with success very early in its career. If it suffers disappointment after disappointment in the early days it is all too easily convinced it can't catch what ever has been flushed for it and therefore it either doesn't try so hard or doesn't try at all. However, the latter stages of the hawk's training should have indicated to the falconer just what level of fitness the hawk has reached and if there was any doubt as to its capabilities to pursue quarry then the calling off period could be extended. Calling the hawk to the fist from long distances and giving repeated jump ups from the ground will help get a hawk fit but nothing sharpens the mind or body like the real thing. Chasing quarry takes a hawk into a higher gear and soon tones muscle and quickens the responses. So this is where a catch 22 situation can arise if you are not careful. The hawk needs to chase quarry to get truly fit but needs to catch quarry to keep its interest and reactions honed which it can't really do well until it is fit. This is precisely why such care should be taken when trying to get the hawk entered.

A hen pheasant that wasn't as fast as she thought.

Let us assume the hawk has attained a reasonable degree of fitness and the time is considered right to try and make a start on its, hopefully, successful hunting career. Depending on what quarry species will be the mainstay of any future hunting, then this is the one that should be sought out and selective slips looked for. Let us look at pheasant and rabbit as two prime examples as they are after all the backbone of hawking in Great Britain at this time.

Taking pheasants first; it is obvious that the hawk is going to need a very close slip to give it any realistic chance of success. What you are looking for in the very early days is not so much sporting flights but successful ones. Once two or three kills have been achieved and the hawk knows it is truly capable of tackling a particular quarry then you can progress onto quality sporting flights. But in early days the process of entering is about the sport that is to come, not what is being experienced at the time. What will be required initially are chances that more or less guarantee the hawk contact with the pheasant. If you are using a pointing dog with your hawk then you are off to a very good start and if you have made your hawk

to the hood then things are looking even better. Before explaining how I wou
entering process let me say that should the hawk in question not be used to d
the hood then all is not lost. It will probably just be a lot harder and require a
luck. After all, without the aid of a dog there will be no pre-warning of a phe_____ bursting
from cover and it may happen right at your feet or it may happen 15 yards away.

In such circumstances I would take my hawk and dog out in search of a good slip and I
would then call the hawk to the fist two or three times from either fence posts or trees to get
its mind focused on the glove and eating. Then I would run my dog in an area where I knew
I stood a very good chance of finding a pheasant. The hawk having had two or three focusing
flights would then be hooded on my fist so as not to have it distracted by all and sundry
around it. Once the dog is steady on a good point and I had made sure it was a pheasant, the
hawk would be unhooded and allowed to settle for a few moments to regain its composure
completely. If the hawk looked or acted at all distracted then I would give it a morsel of food
just to get its attention back. Once this was done I would then walk slowly in towards the
pointing dog trying as hard as possible to ensure that the pheasant didn't break until the last
possible second. If luck was with us then we would be at the stage of almost standing on it
before it suddenly hurtles up from the cover it was hiding in. If all goes to plan, which in
actual fact doesn't often happen, then the hawk has only to launch itself from the fist and grab
the pheasant before it is really up and flying properly. Should it do so then get to the hawk as
fast as you can and help subdue the pheasant and despatch it as quickly as possible. If your
hawk fails to take this particular opportunity then move on and try again.

I would call the hawk back to the fist and take a few minutes and sit somewhere nice
and quiet and give the hawk plenty of time to regain its composure. When the hawk was
thoroughly relaxed and settled again I would hood him or her up and move on with the
pointer to find another chance. Should the hawk not have been made to the hood for any
reason then the falconer will just have to ensure that the hawk does not bate off at quarry
it does not stand much chance of catching. If I had two attempts on my first outing and the
hawk had chased both times but failed then I would call it a day and wait till the following
day to try again. If, however, the first one or two occasions had not resulted in the hawk
chasing then I would try once or even twice more the same day. I can well remember many
years ago I was trying to enter a female Harris Hawk and she actually bated the other way
and went up a tree the first three times pheasants were flushed for her. But the fourth time
of asking she grabbed the pheasant and from that point we never looked back. What was
different about flush number four to the other three I have no idea, but something was
different for her and once she was switched on to catching pheasants she would then chase
them as if her life depended on it.

Sooner or later your hawk will grab one of the pheasants that are flushed and when
it does so help her despatch it and then give her a really good feed up on the warm flesh.
Remember that we fly for sport but the hawk flies to eat. Consequently, her ultimate reward
is a crop of food, let her take her time and really enjoy the meal. Refit her equipment whilst
she is pluming her prey and tie her leash to your hawking vest or telemetry bag. Let her really
enjoy herself for a while, treat the first three or four kills in this way and let the hawk know

Eight

An adult female Harris Hawk that has caught a rabbit bolted for it by ferrets.

that catching quarry is a very good thing for her. But be careful not to err on the side of only offering easy slips for too long. Once she has achieved three or four easy kills then move on and start hawking properly. For example, just stand off from the pointer a little and then flush the pheasant so that the hawk has to actually chase now as opposed to simply leap from the fist. The transition from entering to actual hawking should be done as soon as the falconer is certain that the hawk is confident and is off in pursuit of a pheasant the second it bursts from cover. The good thing is that most young Harris Hawks will be brought to the entering process just as the pheasant hawking season is beginning. Therefore, the odds are that several of the initial slips will be at young birds which will help the situation.

There are two things I definitely don't do when I am trying to enter a hawk in the circumstances I have described above. The first is to allow the hawk to take stand in a tree close to where the dog is on point and allow it to take the pheasant on from there. Even if I intend to let the hawk follow on when real hunting commences, I do not want it killing from anywhere other than the fist in the early days. The hawk needs to think that I'm an essential part of the hunting equation and the last thought that I want to put in its mind is that it is better off away from me than with me. The other thing that I never do in the early days is cast the hawk off at quarry. If it doesn't want to chase at that particular moment then hurling it into the air will actually not help the situation at all and is a negative thing for the hawk to experience – better to be patient and wait for the next opportunity. Not always easy in the heat of the moment but better for your relationship with the hawk in the long run.

In the case of entering to rabbits then the procedure will be a little different. If you are walking rabbits up, then the hawk needs to be unhooded from the moment you think there is a chance of flushing something for it. I would still give the hawk two or three flights to the fist just to get it focused on yourself and food before beginning to hunt in earnest. Once her attention is in the direction you want it, the search for a rabbit can begin. Try to find one in a situation that should prove advantageous to her. Not always easy I know but try and go to somewhere you know that any rabbits there will be out in the open or have a long way to run to cover. Just as with the pheasants, don't be too surprised or alarmed if your hawk simply watches the first two or three rabbits run away without making any effort to go after them. I cannot offer an explanation as to why it should be so but this does happen quite often. Sooner or later it will chase and hopefully before too long it will make a kill. When it does then feed it up and let it know that putting in the effort to chase is a very worthwhile thing. The whole secret of training hawks and dogs is to enforce positive actions and keep negative ones to a minimum.

When entering a hawk to rabbits it is probably far easier to accomplish the desired result by ferreting, this way you can select a small bury and one that is in the open. You can position yourself so that the hawk has the best possible advantage for any flight that may ensue.

Finally, let me say that I have never found it necessary to reduce a Harris Hawk in weight from its normal response weight to get it to fly quarry. If it doesn't immediately chase all and sundry at the very first time of asking don't withhold food that day and think this will make it super keen the following day. If the response of the hawk to your fist or your voice is immediate then its weight is about right. It certainly does not need reducing. As soon as the hawk is killing, you will find that its weight can go up a bit. By chasing quarry hard the hawk will be burning lots of energy and building muscle. Your intention should be to fly the hawk in as high a condition as possible that still allows the hawk to be obedient.

chapter nine
hunting

T he sport of falconry is hunting wild quarry in its natural state with a trained hawk. So
that is what we have been working towards since we took our hawk on the fist for
the very first time. Our initial training and entering have been completed and now it's
time to actually hunt as often as we can with our hawk and to achieve good quality flights.
The aim for most falconers will be to enjoy some excellent sport and this will take preference
over merely killing for the sake of it. Whilst a good fit confident hawk will be successful and
therefore kill well, the emphasis should always be on the quality of the flying and not the
quantity.

When it comes to hunting successfully, weight control becomes absolutely vital, as
does understanding what takes weight from your hawk and what adds it. This may sound so
blatantly obvious as to be not worth bothering about, but there are many factors, other than
sheer quantity of food that can affect the weight of a hawk. For instance, any single weight can
actually have three different interpretations. For example, let us take a female Harris Hawk
that weighs two pounds. Is she two pounds and rising, is she two pounds static or is she two
pounds on the way down from a higher weight? My favourite old female Harris, Maud, is a
good example of how weight can vary with the same hawk. At the beginning of the season
when she has been properly enseamed after the moult she will start taking quarry at around
two pounds three ounces. Once she is back to full fitness and killing well her weight can be
allowed to creep up until she is flying another two to three ounces heavier. I normally end my
season with a few weeks in Scotland hunting rabbits and at that time of year it is very cold and
I give my hawk a full crop of warm rabbit most days when she has killed. The combination
of hard flying and cold weather conditions means that I can happily keep her at her very top
flying weight of two pounds seven ounces and know that she will fly quarry just as hard as
ever. But rabbit is not one of the most nutritious foods and therefore she can eat in bulk and
not put on too much weight. If I were to give her the equivalent weight of rats, mice, game bird
or beef then her weight would shoot up and she would also become sluggish in her reactions.
Also, if I were to try and fly her at anywhere near this weight at the beginning of the season
then I would undoubtedly have great problems getting her back on the fist if she missed her
quarry. She would be far too independent at this weight and I would realistically have very
little control over her.

It is very easy to get lulled into a false sense of security regarding the weight of your
hawk. With the Harris Hawk there is no need to screw their weight down to get them entered

Adult female Harris Hawk soaring. One of the most rewarding ways to hunt with these ubiquitous hawks.

and hunting well. With many species of raptor it is the normal practice to get them flying free and then just drop a little more off of their weight in an effort to get them that little keener and instantly interested in quarry. In fact, in most cases with the Harris Hawk the exact opposite is true. As soon as the hawk is starting to put on muscle the falconer can let the weight go up at least an ounce, in the case of a female, and she will normally hunt more determinedly.

Every falconer wants to fly his hawk as heavy as possible, consistent with the hawk being obedient to the fist and instantly ready to tackle any flight opportunity that presents itself. If you take a look at two hawks that at the point of being entered to quarry weighed exactly the same, but one is only flown at weekends and the other is flown almost daily, then looking at them again at the end of the season would be quite surprising to most beginners. The hawk that is flown everyday will normally be in better condition with regard to feather bloom and colour of cere and on the feet. It will fly an ounce or two higher than its weekend counterpart and will take on much longer and harder slips. Generally speaking it will be considerably fitter and have much more confidence in the field, it will look and be a better hawk altogether. That is not to say that the weekend only hawk won't be any good – far from it. But it will not have anywhere near the confidence or the experience that the hawk that is flown daily will have gained.

The Harris Hawk is so unique and truly adaptable that it can be hunted successfully in one of several different ways, or even a combination of them. 'Off the fist' is as the name implies

A successful outcome for this adult female.

flying at quarry that has been spotted whilst the hawk is still on the fist and this can either be walked up, pointed with a dog or ferreted. Falconers that prefer this type of hawking seem to do so for a couple of reasons. Firstly, they are in total control of what quarry the hawk is or isn't slipped at. Secondly, the falconer feels he is far more a part of the proceedings than when a hawk is following on.

Following on is supposedly when the falconer works cover with or without the aid of a dog, and the hawk follows on, normally from tree to tree, as the falconer progresses. I say supposedly because all too often the reality of this type of flying is that the falconer runs after the hawk and takes it back up onto the fist after it has killed something. I well remember going out with quite a well known falconer to see his cast of female Harris Hawks hunting.

As we entered a large wood the first hawk, then the other one was allowed to fly up into a tree. Having landed on their respective vantage points both hawks were off within a few seconds of each other and worked their way from tree-to-tree through the wood. After a while they both flew off with what was obviously serious intention and we eventually found them on a rabbit. The wood was a large one and had good cover and we needed telemetry to find the hawks on their kill. To me this just wasn't what falconry is supposed to be about. Other than when the hawks left the fist and then the trees we hadn't seen them until we tracked them down again. We hadn't seen or had the opportunity to enjoy the flight. I commented on this and was told that this was real sport – if it truly is then it is time I did something else.

Soaring is another very effective method of hunting with a Harris Hawk and it is something they do a great deal of in the wild. In their native habitat they tend to use thermals

Allowing the hawk to feed up after a good kill.

to help them soar and accordingly this method of hunting requires very little energy on their part. They just let the hot air do the hard work for them. In Britain we don't tend to have too many days where soaring on hot air thermals is possible but we do have plenty of opportunity for our hawks to soar on the wind. When I lived in Scotland surrounded by hills, which were inhabited by generous numbers of rabbits and blue hares, this was without doubt my favourite method of hunting with my Harris.

Many people find enjoyment in flying their Harris Hawks in a group and I have often seen up to five Harris Hawks being slipped at the same rabbit. Hawking is a very personal thing and what is meat to one man is very definitely poison to another. I have to say that flying several Harris Hawks together at the same quarry does absolutely nothing to me other than inwardly hope the quarry gets away. There are those that say this type of flying reflects the true natural hunting method of the Harris Hawk in the wild. To a certain degree this is true, but then circumstances are a great deal different in an arid region of Mexico or Peru where quarry is extremely scarce and where the family of Harris Hawks will go hungry if they don't co-operate in their hunting. The shire counties of England and rabbits bolted with the aid of ferrets does not to my mind offer a comparison that will stand very close scrutiny. As I say though each to their own. I prefer one hawk or even in certain circumstances a cast of hawks to be slipped at quarry.

Let's go back and look at the various methods in a little more detail starting with 'Off the fist'. To my mind this is the most basic way of hunting with a hawk, any sort of hawk, and probably one of the two methods that has given me the most satisfaction over the years. The falconer walks through cover or over ground that he thinks will hold quarry and slips the hawk at anything suitable that gets up within range and sufficiently away from cover. If it is felt that the hawk has a reasonable chance of success then it is slipped, if not then it is held back. If the falconer holds onto the jesses and only releases them when he has made the judgement call as to whether the flight is a good one or not there will be opportunities that are missed. It can happen that the hawk will bate because it has seen something the falconer hasn't. As the falconer hasn't seen what the hawk has he holds onto the jesses and the hawk hangs upside down. By the time the hawk has regained the fist, the quarry will have sufficient head start to make good its escape.

I think that to lose some flights like this is completely acceptable, because it will never really amount to a significant number, and the positive thing is that the falconer retains complete control. The hawk never ever gets into the mode of self hunting and picking the flights it wants. In certain circumstances the falconer can allow the hawk some free reign and go off from the fist when it chooses. For example, if the falconer and hawk are going through some patches of scrub and the hawk goes into characteristic quarry spotting mode. That is where the hawk stands tall on the fist and keeps craning its neck to look down. When a Harris Hawk acts like this you are more or less certain that it is aware that something is on the ground close to it and you should anticipate that a flight could, quite literally, erupt at your feet at any moment.

When ferrets are being used to flush rabbits for the hawk then flying from the fist means that there are no accidents regarding the hawk and ferret. Not that this is normally too much of a problem, hawks will very quickly learn what a ferret is and ignore them but it is always better to be safe than sorry. The time that a ferret is at risk from a hawk, even one that has worked with them constantly, is when the hawk is on the ground and the ferret sticks its head up out of the hole. Sometimes, a rabbit doesn't bolt cleanly and merely pops out of one hole and goes straight back down the one next to it. The hawk has left the fist and lands on the ground but is too late to grab the rabbit. It then peers into the hole and the ferret starts to shuffle out. The hawk's reactions are such that it could foot the ferret before it realises exactly what is emerging from the hole. In such a situation it is imperative to get the hawk back up on the fist as quickly as possible.

It is useful when wanting to use ferrets to have someone with you to take care of that side of things. But, it is not impossible to manage both the ferreting and the hawking on your own and still only slip the hawk from the fist. It just requires careful planning to ensure that things go smoothly and this is yet another occasion where being able to hood the hawk can help. Having someone else to do the ferreting is not always the blessing you may well think it's going to be. I can remember getting invited out on a club field meet a few years back, it was mid-February and five falconers gathered at a farm that looked like a good place to ferret and hawk. A supposedly willing volunteer had come along to do the ferreting for the hawking group and was keen to make a start as quickly as possible. Flying order was quickly established and it was definitely a one hawk at a time slipping situation.

The first group of holes were ferreted and a bolted rabbit was duly caught by the hawk whose turn it was to be slipped. Whilst the hawk was being taken up the ferreter moved on to the next set of holes and without waiting for anybody to come to him, introduced two ferrets. As the group of falconers approached the holes several rabbits bolted and although the hawk that was next up did catch one, it was more by luck than by judgement. The field leader quietly tried to suggest that the ferreter should just hang on and let the group catch up after each flight. He was promptly told that it was up to the falconers to keep up with the ferrets and moved on. The day disintegrated into a bit of a farce after that and consequently ended early. So, having your own ferreter doesn't always pay although generally it can be a plus point.

When you are hunting with the aid of a dog the hawk very soon learns to take notice of it and what it's doing. Any Harris Hawk worth its keep soon realises what role the dog plays in providing flights and accordingly will learn to recognise the tell tale signs that indicate quarry is present. In the off the fist situation the hawk will tighten its feathers in anticipation of a flight as the falconer carefully and quietly approaches the dog. If there is a breeze blowing then the falconer will approach the dog from behind so that the hawk is facing directly into the wind. If the wind is strong then the approach is better made across the wind so as to give the hawk a decent chance.

All too often people make unfair comparisons between the flying and hunting abilities of Goshawks and Harris Hawks. They are completely different raptors and hunt in a different way. The one thing that a Harris can't do, and at which a Goshawk excels, is power directly into the wind. The design and physical make up of the Harris Hawk does not allow it to do so, so care and consideration should be given to wind direction if it is blowing with any strength. If in such a situation as described above you approach the dog across and slightly up wind at least the hawk has a good chance of catching its prey before it can turn directly into it.

I really cannot understand why anybody would want to hunt a hawk such as a Harris without the aid of a dog. Good dog work is a joy to watch and as I get older I get as much pleasure from seeing a well trained dog work as I do seeing a good hawk hunt well. It makes no difference whether it is a pointer that indicates game for the hawk or a spaniel that finds and flushes it the work is still pleasant to watch. To be able to be part of a three-way team on a daily basis is one of the major appeals of hunting with a Harris Hawk for me. As often as not the falconer will be the one that sometimes feels the odd one out as hawk and dog work together with a very clear mutual understanding of each others role.

Following on is a very pleasant way to hunt with your hawk and one that would well suit those that are unable to use either a dog or ferrets to assist with finding quarry. The idea is a simple enough one. The hawk is trained to follow the falconer, particularly through woods, as he endeavours to find quarry at which the hawk can fly. Every now and then the hawk is called back to the fist by the falconer or encouraged to change position by the falconer calling and waving his glove in the air. The hawk is not given, nor should expect, a reward each time it is called down to the fist. As well as the falconer being free to rigorously beat bushes and undergrowth the hawk will have the advantage of height should something be flushed as a result of his endeavours. If the hawk is well trained and obedient then following on can be an extremely pleasant and rewarding way in which to hunt with a Harris Hawk.

What is not so pleasant is when the hawk dictates the strategy and direction the hunting will take because it has been allowed too much free reign and is, to all intents and purposes, self hunting. This means in practical terms that the hawk, once it has left the fist of the falconer, is going where and when it wants and the falconer ends up doing the following on. I have even been out with one falconer and hawk where the hawk could only ever be recovered if it killed or with the use of a lure. This is not my idea of hawking. I want to be part of the hawking and have control, as much as it is possible to do so, of the proceedings.

Providing the hawk is obedient and does follow on then a dog can be run underneath her as well. I often hunt my male Harris Hawks like this and have had some superb flights, especially at pheasants. I stress the point that the hawk should return to the fist when it is proffered so that the falconer always remains in control. There will be occasions when it is advantageous to the hawk to be in a tree and have some height over the quarry that is about to be flushed for it. Equally there will be times when you want the hawk on the fist in anticipation of the flush. The last thing you want on such an occasion is a hawk that only comes down to the fist reluctantly after much shouting and calling. There is no need for the hawk to be screwed right down in weight to make it attentive and responsive, in fact almost the opposite is true. You want the hawk to be working both on its own initiative and in conjunction with yourself and your dog. Care and attention to basic obedience should bring about the desired result.

One of my favourite methods of hunting my own Harris Hawks is soaring. It is a hunting strategy that the species regularly adopts in the wild and its wing loading is ideally suited to it. It's simplicity itself to encourage a Harris Hawk to soar and requires only regular access to a wind facing slope. The falconer positions himself on the slope and faces into the wind and the hawk is then encouraged to take to the air and the falconer then walks down the slope, which will have the effect of encouraging the hawk to fly directly into the wind. By flying into the wind the hawk will find it easy to rise on outstretched wings and will have to circle to keep the falconer within a relatively close proximity. As with all things the trick in teaching a newly trained hawk to soar is not to try and rush things too much. Take each stage carefully and aim for a small degree of improvement each time the hawk is flown. But in actual fact once the hawk has been soaring for a few days it makes very rapid progress all by itself. When the hawk first soars then let her just circle you once and then call her down to the fist for a small reward. The next time let her circle slightly longer, and so on. In no time at all she will be circling several times and normally rising as she does so.

As soon as she is fairly competent at soaring try and get her a decent slip as soon as possible. The quicker she learns that a combination of height and being attentive to the falconer brings a reward the sooner the real hunting can begin. None of my Harris Hawks have gone particularly high, some 100 to a 120 feet probably being the highest, but then they don't really need to. When I lived near to Grantown on Spey in Scotland, I had the good fortune to live on the edge of an excellent grouse moor. The moor itself consisted of three hills that ran one into another and therefore I had a selection of slopes that meant that some of them would always be right with regard to the wind for hawking. The moor had plenty of blue hares on it and where it butted up against arable land there was a healthy rabbit population. This meant that from a falconer's point of view there was always quarry to be found for the hawk. Nothing succeeds like success and because I could produce quarry on a daily basis for my hawks they got better and better as the season progressed.

Always empty the bladder of a freshly caught rabbit straight away.

Once a Harris Hawk is truly fit and adept at soaring you will be surprised just how long it will spend on the wing following the dog and falconer as they work below it trying to provide a flight. My only word of caution would be to make sure you still call the hawk down to the fist on a regular basis. Just like the following on method of hunting the falconer needs to be the one in charge of the situation, not the hawk.

Group flying has no appeal to me although I can see what the attraction is to others. It is certainly is an extremely sociable way of going hawking. I personally prefer to see just one hawk chase most of the quarry species we have available here in Great Britain. I have flown a cast of males myself and thoroughly enjoyed it and have also flown a female of mine in company with another one. Hawking, as with any pursuit, is a personal thing and my own preferences lie with flying just one hawk at a time. This is not to say I think that those who choose to group hawk are wrong, it is just that it holds no appeal for me.

Most Harris Hawks are happy to fly with each other and although there will be minor squabbles over prey occasionally, normally this never develops into anything more serious. There are some hawks that cannot be trusted with others and these normally give off plenty of warning signs that it would be unwise to fly them in company, even if it is of their own kind. I have often seen five females flown together and also a group of four consisting of two males and two females. In my own, admittedly limited, experience of group flying this is where the potential for a problem could possibly lie. The stronger and more powerful females will often try and move the male out of the way if it is on the kill first.

Another method of flying the Harris Hawk that I have absolutely no time for at all is lamping. Again I am not decrying the method or those that employ it but merely stating it is not for me. As mentioned previously I want to be an integral part of the hawking I do and lamping does nothing for me – if I wanted to hunt with a lamp I would buy a lurcher.

By the very nature of the sport there will be times when a hawk is lost, albeit temporarily. The advent of decent telemetry systems has made the permanent loss of a Harris Hawk almost a thing of the past. There will be occasions when even telemetry won't help in the recovery of a hawk but these tend to be few and far between, but to fly without telemetry in this day and age is unforgivable. The cost of systems has come down sufficiently to the point where they are no longer beyond anyone's reach. I can think of several instances where I have been searching for a hawk and have actually been within 100 metres of it, but without telemetry I would have struggled to locate it.

Telemetry should not be used as a short cut to training a hawk properly. Never be tempted to fly a hawk before it is really ready simply because you can put a transmitter on it should things go wrong. Any tracking system is meant to be an aid to the falconer not a means of by passing any stage of the basic training of the hawk. Also, don't abandon the old skills and field craft associated with tracking a lost hawk just because we do have modern systems. There will be times when telemetry can and will let you down. Whether it is because batteries have failed in either the receiver or transmitter or perhaps the aerial has become detached from the transmitter. For what ever reason it is useful to be able to fall back on the more traditional skills associated with locating a lost hawk. Being able to understand the signs that nature gives off will always be of use. Rooks, crows and magpies mobbing and generally becoming agitated, song birds giving alarm calls, or pigeons suddenly veering in the sky. Should you lose a hawk then inform as many people as you can as quickly as possible. Police, local radio stations and newspapers, gamekeepers and land owners. There are also two organisations that help with the recovery of lost hawks so get in touch with these as quickly as possible, but should you get your hawk back don't forget to let all these people know with equal haste that it has been recovered.

The other thing is never give up hope. I lost my old favourite Maud for three months in her second season and after three or four weeks or so I had given up hope of ever seeing her again. But she reappeared one day when I was out walking the dogs and actually came down to the fist having hit it and then flown on several times. I didn't have a glove with me at the time and had wrapped part of a jumper over my hand, nor did I have any food but she eventually came down anyway. Fortunately for me she still had her permanent flying jesses in place and I was able to hang onto her and get her home. She was five ounces heavier than when I had lost her so it wasn't desperation for food that had brought her back to me.

It would be a mistake on my part to move on from a chapter on hunting without a few words regarding the quarry. The falconer should always treat anything his hawk catches with the utmost respect and do his best to ensure it is despatched as quickly and as painlessly as possible. As sportsmen and women we have a duty to be ethical in the pursuit of our sport and make sure that quarry is treated with the respect it deserves.

chapter ten
diet & the moult

Head study of a ten year old male Harris Hawk.

T he moult is a perfectly natural process that takes place each year whereby the hawk completely changes its plumage and the main flight feathers, such as primaries and tail feathers are moulted in pairs. A pair of feathers will be dropped by the hawk and when the replacements are almost fully down the next pair will drop, and so on. In Harris Hawks the innermost pair of primaries are dropped first, then working outwards the next pair will follow and then the next until finally the outer pair are the last of all to be changed. With the tail it is the centre pair of feathers, known as the deck feathers, which will drop first and then in turn outwards from there and this process continues until all the major flight feathers have been changed. The moult usually begins somewhere between mid March till early April and will last through till September or even in some cases early October. In the case of passage hawks the first moult will be somewhat erratic and the hawk may well not change all of its flight feathers. There are various drugs available that will accelerate the moult and their use is supposedly increasing in popularity in America. But, to me, I cannot see the point in trying to rush a natural process whose conclusion will coincide with the availability of quarry for the hawk once more.

There are three different options for the falconer to choose from when it comes to moulting his hawk. The first is to carry on flying the hawk and more or less ignore the fact that the hawk is indeed moulting. This is perfectly acceptable as long as the quantity and quality of the food being fed to the hawk is increased. The hawk will not only to need to replace the energy used in flying as it would normally, but also for the growth of the new feathers. Failure to allow for this extra burden on the hawk's system could result in hunger traces on the new plumage. These are very thin lines across the webbing and shaft of the feathers and are in actual fact weak points that will break easily if put under any strain.

Most of the quarry species readily available to the Harris Hawk will be breeding at the time of the moult and so the normal practice is to stop flying the hawk for the six month period. If it is decided to put the hawk down and moult it out then there are two ways of doing this. The hawk can either be moulted at the bow or it can be turned loose and moulted in an aviary. Both methods have their advantages and disadvantages and both achieve the desired result come September. So it really is a matter of whatever suits the falconer and their particular circumstances best.

If moulted at the bow then this means the hawk is handled daily and can be fed on the fist to keep it manned. The weight of the hawk can still be increased but it will retain its tameness throughout the moult. The daily routine of taking the hawk in and out of the hawk house and weighing it will ensure that the hawk retains its good manners and its calmness. But as it is not being flown at quarry it will need some exercise and also some distraction to help keep it occupied. It is therefore a good idea to still jump the hawk to the fist for its food and to give plenty of tirings to keep it amused as well as helping to keep the beak in trim. The tirings should be particularly tough and should be given to the hawk when he or she is put out on the bow in the mornings. Obviously, this is after having ensured that the hawk has cast. If not then simply wait for the pellet to be disgorged and then give the tiring. This can take the form of a stump of either a pigeon or a ducks wing which has been severed at the shoulder joint. The feathers are then removed from the tiring and any meat other than flecks that have been left on the bone. The hawk will then happily pick at the skin and sinews for a considerable time. Another good tiring is backbone of rabbit that has had the majority of the meat removed from it.

Once the hawk has got into a routine of having a tiring each day you will be surprised how quickly they get to look forward to it. As well as helping to keep the beak in trim and the hawk occupied, a great many muscles will be involved in the process of cleaning up the tiring. Chicken necks from the butchers also used to be ideal for this purpose but with all the things that are added to poultry these days I prefer to stick to wild duck and pigeon wings. Pheasant wings can also be used but they need to be cleaned very thoroughly of any meat.

The alternative to moulting the hawk at the bow is to turn it loose in an aviary. Most

A young male on a bow perch that has seen better days.

Myra leaves the fist in pursuit of a rabbit.

people who intend to do this stuff their hawks full of food for several days and then simply put them loose in the aviary. This is not really the best way of going about things and it is far better to very gradually increase the weight of the hawk for 10 days or so before it goes into the aviary. During which time the hawk should be cast and have its beak and talons coped quite hard. I always make a point of changing the anklets and fitting very thin permanent flying jesses so that it should not prove to be a major trauma if I wish to catch the hawk up at anytime. I prefer to put my hawks into a wire fronted aviary so that they can see plenty going on around them all the time. They are intelligent and sociable creatures and should not be shut away where they see nothing happening day after day. I also feel it is not a good idea to let them get horrendously overweight. I much prefer to give them slightly more than their daily flying rations, bearing in mind their weight was already moderately increased before they were turned loose in the aviary. A bath should be placed in the aviary and the water should be changed on a regular basis. Therefore, it is a good idea to plan your aviary so that this can be done without having to unduly disturb the hawk to do so.

Providing you go into the aviary on a regular basis and give the hawk its food from the glove a certain degree of tameness will be maintained. Harris Hawks are not like accipiters and do not seem to forget all their training the minute their weight is increased or they are not handled daily. If the hawk is kept at a reasonable weight and will come to the fist inside the

My old girl Maud in her 13th year.

aviary without too much bother then it can be jessed up and put out on the lawn occasionally and the aviary given a quick clean and tidy up. Six months is a long time and there will be plenty that needs cleaning. If you feed by food tray or food chute onto a platform then ensure that these are kept as clean as is possible under the circumstances. Also, the opportunity can be taken to pick up intact flight feathers and store them away in case they should ever be required for imping.

Taking a hawk up from the moult needs to be given a little thought and should be planned to a certain degree. A decision needs to be taken as to exactly when the hawk will be handled again and then about 10 days beforehand its food intake can be decreased. As well as the quantity of food being reduced, so should the quality. For approximately the first four days feed the hawk on lightly washed meat with no casting what so ever. Washed meat is beef that has been held under a tap and had water run over for a couple of minutes. It is then dried thoroughly and is ready to give to the hawk, then on the fifth day give a normal meal of quail or rat with casting. On the days the hawk is being fed washed meat try and feed her early in the day, around noon if possible. Then in the evening when the meat from the crop would have passed down into the stomach, more correctly known as the panel, give the hawk some rangle. Rangle is just small smooth round pebbles about the size of a pea. What they do is stir and break up the grease and internal slime that has formed in the panel and intestines of the hawk. I normally give six stones to a male Harris and eight to a female.

If you have a hawk that is placid by nature then hood her up and then the stones can be gently slipped down into her crop one at a time. If the hawk kicks up a fuss then it may have to be cast to administer the rangle. Ensure that when you are popping rangle down the throat of a hawk that you miss the windpipe opening which is behind the tongue. Once the rangle has been given carry the hawk on the fist for a few minutes to ensure that it isn't immediately cast back up again. Give the rangle to the hawk for around a week, but not on the days when you give the hawk casting with its food. The stones will pass through the system and can be picked up the following morning from underneath the perch of the hawk. Do not give any more rangle until all previous stones have been accounted for, they can then be thoroughly washed and used again. This internal cleansing process is known as enseaming and is something that is largely overlooked by modern falconers. Once the hawk has been cleansed internally then normal training and dieting can commence. There is a very old adage that runs: "Washed meats and stones maketh a hawk to fly; long fasting and much casting will cause a hawk to die".

Keeping a supply of top quality food to hand is not the problem it once was. With specialist suppliers it is possible to pick up the phone and order a whole range of food products for your hawk. These will include quail, chicks, rats, mice, hamsters, guinea pigs and rabbits. All of which are good food but have different values when it comes to protein levels and how they will affect your hawk's weight. Added to these will be beef from the butchers and of course quarry taken by the hawk. The one possible food source that should be avoided at all costs is road kills. Even if you witness something killed by a car in front of you or kill it yourself, you don't know if it was hit because it had slow reactions due to being ill in the first place. The risk is just not worth taking.

Day old chicks probably form the basis of the diet that most Harris Hawks in Britain get fed. They are a good all round food and hawks fed on them tend to get nice yellow feet and cere and this is due to the carotene that is found in the yolk of the chick. Chicks have the same nutritional value as beef and the two can be alternated to give a reasonable diet, particularly if interspersed with other foods. When feeding chicks I like to add a food supplement and personally use a product called 'Raptor Essentials'. But there are several others on the market and probably all do the same job. I am happy with the product I use as it is simple to use, has a long date life, can be obtained easily and obviously my hawks do well on it. Added to that is the fact that it is not expensive.

Rabbit is a good natural food, especially for Harris Hawks and if fed warm is a good food, but once frozen and then defrosted it seems to lose much of its goodness. But it does mean that you can feed your hawk a large crop without it putting weight on. If feeding defrosted rabbit then it doesn't hurt to just add a drop of cod liver oil to it. Hawks will happily ingest this and it seems to do their digestive system good.

Hare and venison are good rich dark meats and high in protein. They should be fed sparingly otherwise a hawk will very soon put on weight and get above herself.

Mice and rats are both extremely good food and are high in nutrition. I always gut rats and remove half of the body fur so as to minimise the risk of impacted crop. The mice I feed whole, but some hawks do not like rodents and will only eat them if really hungry.

Quail are excellent food; high in nutrition and I have only ever had one hawk that was not keen on them. They are extremely useful for bringing up the condition of a hawk quickly and I feed them a great deal to hawks that are moulting. They are considerably more expensive than most other types of food but well worth the outlay. Pheasant and partridge are very similar foods.

chapter eleven
common mistakes

E verybody, no matter how long they have been a practising falconer, will make mistakes when it comes to training and flying a hawk. It stands to reason that those that are relatively new to the sport are vulnerable to making more mistakes than those with some experience under their belts. Or at least that's the way logic says it should be. Most mistakes can be avoided with a little forethought but sometimes the would-be falconer does not have sufficient knowledge to realise his actions are building a fault into his hawk's behaviour until it is too late. These mistakes in training or daily handling will lead to the hawk developing an irritating habit or one that is inconvenient to the falconer.

Many such mistakes can be corrected at a later stage by careful management of the hawk and redirecting certain behaviour patterns. But all too often a mistake on the falconer's part can lead to either serious injury or death on the part of the hawk. With this in mind and not because I enjoy being a harbinger of doom and gloom, I will run through some of those that I have come across over the years. Because it is easy to pick holes in other people's behaviour whilst lauding your own I will start with two very stupid errors made by myself. I hope that by relaying them and other examples to the reader the same mistakes will not be made over and over by other falconers to come.

The first concerns hooding. As I mentioned in the chapter on hooding it is important to make a hawk to the hood in its early stages of training. The hood must be introduced whilst the hawk is still very wary of you and is literally more disturbed by your presence than anything else. This is even more essential when it comes to training a falcon than a hawk. When I first set out on the road to become a falconer my first ever hawk was, in fact, a small passage falcon, a Red Headed Merlin from India. I made the absolutely classic mistake that so many beginners make of not being able to hood the falcon the first few times I tried and obviously each failed attempt ended with the falcon bating from my fist. My thinking then was that other than the hood I was making good progress with the falcon so why risk putting the training back by upsetting it. I would leave the hooding process until the falcon was thoroughly manned. In my mind, at that time, this was a logical thought process and would no doubt eventually bring the desired result. Nothing could have been further from the truth and once the falcon was thoroughly manned it concentrated all its efforts on avoiding being hooded. Because it was so well manned by the time I tried hooding lessons again it didn't even bother to bate from the hood but merely did repeated snake impressions by bobbing and weaving its head or tucking its head into its shoulders.

Adult female Harris Hawk on kill.

The truth of the matter was that I never could hood this little falcon successfully and as a result it impeded a great many things. I flew the Red Head off of the fist at starlings and because I couldn't hood him he would often bate at groups of starlings I didn't want to slip him at which was a waste of his energy. I couldn't be anywhere near as selective in his slips as I wanted to be for the fact that he could see what to him was potential quarry and bate at it. The flicker of his wings would alert any groups of starlings in the vicinity and therefore many opportunities were needlessly lost. Also, transporting and not being able to shield the falcon from certain sights caused problems now and again, all of which could have been avoided with introducing and persevering with the hood at the appropriate time in training.

Some years ago I was given a seven year old male Harris Hawk that had never been hooded. He had been used purely for display work and his previous owner felt that hooding him was just not necessary. When he came to me I wanted to be able to hood him and I also wanted to try and get him hunting. The second desire was not dependent on the first but it would make life easier. With a lot of care and attention plus a considerable amount of patience

I managed to get the hawk used to the hood. I am not saying he hoods perfectly but he doesn't bate away from the hood or tuck his head down into his shoulders to avoid it. However, should I hesitate or be in any way indecisive when hooding him then he will turn away from the hood. Then it becomes imperative to get it on at the next attempt or he will start to play up. Accordingly, I hood him carefully but still much more quickly than I would normally any other of my hawks. I bring the hood up into view and over his head all in one movement. This particular hawk is still with me and hunting well I'm glad to say.

Something I haven't actually come across with hawks but can happen is that they get lost with their hoods on. I know of two separate incidents where this happened with falcons though and it is something that should be considered and guarded against. On both occasions a hooded falcon was put down for a few moments whilst the falconers concerned dealt with something else. The falcons were fitted with jesses only, no leash or swivel. With the first she was put down on a fence rail and a gust of wind was all it took for her to open her wings and be carried away. The only salvation was that the day's hunting was not over and therefore the falcon was still fitted with a telemetry transmitter. A hawk or falcon that goes off with its hood on will follow a more or less predictable route, it will fly until it either bumps into something or simply tires out. This falcon flew for over 40 miles before landing. But, thankfully, the telemetry meant we could find her and rescue her before something happened to her. The second falcon only flew a 100 yards or so before hitting a hedgerow and landing on the ground, where she remained until she was picked up. But both incidents could have had far from happy endings.

My next major error in judgement came some 20 odd years later. It involved a male Harris Hawk that was one of the brightest and most intelligent hawks I have ever had the privilege of hunting with. If it hadn't have been for the fact that I caught him up out of the aviary myself, and bled profusely from the attention his parents gave me whilst doing so, I could have been led to believe this hawk had been handled before. I caught him up and fitted his equipment to him on a Saturday evening. The following Friday, just six days later, I flew him loose and he caught a small bird. Not only that but he returned to the fist with it to eat it there.

I had hardly reduced the weight of the hawk at all, he just took to training as if someone had read a falconry book to him. He was entered to rabbits four days after first flying free and was very obedient and a real joy to fly. At the time of working with this particular hawk I was living in Scotland, in the middle of a large estate over which I could hunt at will. At the back of my cottage were my weatherings, kennels and weighing room. Each day I would go to the kennel and let the pointers out and then go and take up the male Harris from his weathering. I would take him into the weighing room, put him on the scales and then fit his telemetry, flying jesses and remove the rest of his equipment. As we emerged from the weighing room I would cast him off into some nearby trees and we would literally start hunting immediately.

Now I would stress at this point that he had been trained to follow on and not the other way round. He followed me, I didn't follow him, but he knew as soon as we came out from the weighing room he would be off and hunting. As we progressed together the hawk became so reliable that I would rarely weigh him. The routine changed and I would merely pick him up from his weathering, fit his gear and off we would go. As soon as we emerged from the

Nice juvenile male Harris Hawk, shame about the bow perch he has to sit on.

Oh so close, but not quite close enough.

weathering I would allow him to take off. I had cast him off into the nearby trees so often that he now automatically headed for them, but this is where I made a rod for my own back.

He was taking the decision as to where he should fly to and when. It took a while for me to notice that he started to bate from the fist as we emerged from the weathering. I went back to weighing him and he would bate as we emerged from the weighing room. He was so used to stepping out of either the weighing room or weathering and then being cast off and flying to the nearby trees that he interpreted this as meaning this was the start of hunting. Therefore, he wanted to get to the trees as quickly as possible, of course, but at the time I could easily remedy the situation in the short term, by use of the hood. But the hawk was not stupid and as soon as he felt me change his mews jesses for field ones he got all fidgety and would dance on the fist until the hood came off. He would then bate and head for the nearest trees. I now hooded him as soon as he was on the fist and didn't unhood him until I was ready for him to start hunting. I made sure that I walked well away from the trees I had been so happy to use in the early days in an effort to try and break the habit, but unfortunately the habit grew to such an extent that he started to bate towards any group of trees we passed.

He retained his obedience to the fist completely and would return instantly regardless of whether any food was proffered, but he spent less and less time on the fist and more and more time flying independently. He still followed on in the truest sense of the meaning, in that he didn't fly ahead but stayed in close proximity to me and whichever pointer or setter I was hunting with. It was just that he preferred to be up a tree or other vantage point rather than on the fist.

We both now live in the other end of the country but his irritating habit, which I built into him, is still with us. He is an excellent hunting hawk and I have enjoyed many splendid flights with him over the years, but I have come to accept that we hunt on his terms because I didn't give enough thought to behaviour patterns that were being formed early in our relationship.

Some of the most common mistakes that are made with hawks relate to equipment, or rather their improper use. I have come across several mistakes which get repeated all too often I'm afraid. The first goes back to hooding and not ensuring that the hood on the hawk fits properly. Just because a hood closes and a hawk cannot see out of it does not mean it's a good fit. A hood that is a perfect fit will meet these criteria but it will also be one that the hawk cannot get off if left alone for any length of time. I have known of several occasions where hawks have been left in the company of other hawks and falcons and an ill-fitting hood has resulted in the death of the nearest neighbour. The circumstances have been varied but the end result is always the same. Some of the scenarios are as follows:- A female Harris Hawk was left hooded on a cadge with a large hybrid falcon. When the owner of the car stopped at a motorway service station the hawk got her hood off and killed the falcon. Another example was a Harris Hawk hooded in the rear of an estate car and an unhooded Merlin perched on the back of the front seat. The Harris Hawk manages to remove its hood and needless to say the Merlin is no more.

I know of an occasion when three falconers were hunting together in Scotland and hawk accommodation was very limited. So a screen perch was hastily erected and three female Harris Hawks were left hooded on the perch at night. All the time they remained hooded the situation was alright but realistically they were too close together for comfort. Sometime during the night the middle hawk got her hood off and killed the other two.

In all the above instances you cannot attach any blame to the hawk that killed another. They were in hunting condition and presented with the opportunity of an easy meal, also, it should be borne in mind that these are examples of the worst case scenarios. The problem is that it's always another hawk or falcon that pays the ultimate price for a falconer not being able to tell if a hood fits properly or not. A hood that does not fit as it should is of no real practical purpose.

The next totally innocent piece of equipment that has led to the death of countless trained hawks is the portable or indoor bow perch. The theory of such perches is absolutely fine. I use them myself and I imagine I will continue to do so for the rest of my falconry career. Such perches are designed so that they can be used more or less anywhere and the falconer will have a means of tethering his hawk safely, particularly when hunting away from home. They come in various sizes and are supposedly designed with certain species in mind. The key to this type of perch is that they are meant to be portable by the falconer but certainly not by the hawk. Under no circumstances should the hawk be able to drag it, no matter how hard she bates. Even on a surface like wet grass the perch should be heavy enough that the hawk cannot shift it. If she can move it then it is either the wrong size or poorly made.

When buying or manufacturing a perch of this kind make sure it really is very substantial and err on the side of excessive weight. After all from the falconer's point of view he is never going to have to move it that much. So better to struggle a little with a really heavy object but have the peace of mind that your hawk cannot move it. If you attend field meets with your hawk check that any hawk on a weathering near yours, which is on a portable perch, cannot move it. If you think there is the slightest chance that it can, then move your hawk. So many hawks have been killed because their neighbour was on one of these portable perches and with constant bating the neighbour has got close enough either to kill or be killed.

The author with an adult female Harris Hawk.

Whilst on the subject of bow perches I saw a hawk lost relatively recently in circumstances I would not have believed if I hadn't seen it with my own eyes. Fortunately, it was recovered unharmed some four hours later, but this was more by luck than judgement. A male Harris Hawk was being taken back to its bow perch on the lawn so as to enjoy the best of the afternoon's sunlight on its back before being put away for the night in its weathering. It had flown well that morning and caught a rabbit, on which it had been fed up, the hawk having a bulging crop and was well satisfied. As the owner approached the bow the Harris Hawk bated towards it and the owner let the leash go. He was still some 10 feet or so from the perch as the Harris landed on the bow with jesses, swivel and leash all fitted.

Needless to say I was aghast and asked what on earth the guy was doing. He stated "it was alright, the hawk always did this on arriving back from hunting". With that the hawk took off with all its equipment trailing behind it. It now sat on the roof of its owner's house with a bulging crop and taking no notice of any efforts at enticing its return. After 30 minutes or

Andy King watches his female Harris Hawk, Myra, closing on a rabbit.

so it took off again and landed in a tree some several hundred yards away. We ran after it and then spent the next three hours or so playing follow the hawk and eventually it flew towards another roof and attempted to land on a television aerial. Luckily for its owner and the future well being of the hawk the trailing leash wrapped itself around part of the aerial and the hawk was caught. It fluttered for a moment or two and then perched precariously. A ladder was hurriedly found and the hawk was soon reunited with its careless owner.

What could have ended up as a slow and lingering death for the hawk turned out to be a stark warning as to what can happen if you get complacent, but I have to tell that the warning hasn't been effectively heeded as I have seen the same falconer doing exactly the same thing with the hawk – that is, allowing it to fly the last few feet to its bow perch with all its equipment fitted. It is without doubt a sad fact that sooner or later the same situation will arise where the hawk goes off with all its equipment, only the next time it might not have such a fortunate ending.

Letting a hawk go with its equipment on is one of the worst possible mistakes a falconer can make. If the hawk is not recovered then it is certain to get caught up and eventually starve to death. That is why I firmly believe that when training a hawk in conjunction with the creance, the line itself should be attached to the slits in the mews jesses rather than to the lower ring of the swivel. Some books go along with this idea, some say attach the creance to the swivel. Others even recommend using a creance that has a snap clip on the end and attaching this clip to the swivel. Any method that leaves the swivel in place is a bad method as far as I am concerned.

The reason I so strongly advocate that the creance be tied to the jesses, and nowhere else, is that the creance line will be a great deal stronger than the leather of the jesses. Should anything give way in this arrangement it will be the slits of the jesses. The hawk will still be able to fly away but at least its legs won't be shackled together. Perhaps at this point I should add that when I have reached the stage where my hawk is being called off on the creance I always fit a telemetry transmitter for the duration of the training session. Then if something were to go wrong I can at least track the hawk and stand a much more realistic chance of getting it back. It is something I have never had to do yet but I consider fitting the transmitter a reasonable safety precaution to take. It requires very little effort and the hawk will have to get used to flying with telemetry at some stage, so it might as well be right from the start. Creance lines that have snap swivels or another type of spring clip arrangement are much too dangerous and are, in my opinion, just an accident waiting to happen. They can jam open, the spring can fail or they can simply come off of the end of the line. To me they just add an element of danger that really need not be there.

No matter what system you use, the point at which to take the greatest care is when the creance has been removed and the swivel and leash are being refitted. When doing so, just take a moment and stand still to do this. I have known of two hawks that have been lost because of owners stumbling in just this sort of situation. Both hawks flew off with swivels fitted, one hawk was undergoing its initial training, the other was an intermewed hawk being reclaimed. Both hawks went off with their day's rations inside them. The young hawk didn't go too far and was eventually found due to the annoyance it was causing amongst the local Magpie population. Despite the food in its crop, which was by no means full, it eventually came down to the fist, but the intermewed hawk was never seen again and it can only be surmised that her end was not a pleasant one.

Both incidents could so easily have been avoided. No one in the entire world is immune from tripping or stumbling with a hawk on the fist. I know for sure that I have in the past and will no doubt do so again sometime in the future. Therefore, just to take two minutes out and stand still whilst refitting a hawk's equipment doesn't seem too unreasonable. Also, in both of these instances the fitting of telemetry would have been of great help. The young hawk would have been found a great deal sooner and telemetry may well have helped find and recover the older hawk.

Another area that should never ever be passed over is the removal of mews jesses and the fitting of flying jesses when out exercising or hunting your hawk. Innumerable hawks have become hung up on fences or in trees before the Aylmeri jess system came into being. Since then there is absolutely no excuse whatsoever for flying a hawk with traditional jesses or Aylmeri anklets with mews jesses still fitted. Whether you prefer to actually swap mews jesses for field jesses or simply remove mews jesses because you have permanent flying jesses fitted is a matter of personal choice. I tend to fit permanent flying jesses for the hunting season. When the season is over and the hawk is going to be allowed to moult I renew the anklets as a matter of course but do not renew the flying jesses as they are simple enough to add again at the start of a fresh season.

I was hawking many years ago with a falconer who did not change the jesses over on his hawk despite having at least two pairs of flying jesses dangling from his hawking bag. Not only was the hawk hunting with mews jesses still in its anklets, it was also doing so without

An adult female Harris Hawk on a hen Pheasant.

a telemetry transmitter fitted. This was at a time when a female Harris Hawk would have cost considerably more than a telemetry set and a couple of decent transmitters. But the falconer in question did actually have a set and good quality transmitters. Apparently, he only ever used them on his falcons. After all, as he told me, "you don't need them on a Harris, they never go anywhere". That remark was probably not a great deal of consolation when we picked up the hawk the following morning. She was hanging from a barbed wire fence and she was dead.

It takes just a couple of minutes to change the jesses over and is not exactly a difficult operation. When I first train my hawks I spend a great deal of time touching their feet and moving the anklets, purely and simply so that in later life they don't want to foot me every time I change their equipment. Also if you have made your hawk to the hood then jobs like this are simplicity itself.

The length of the leash that is allowed once the hawk is tethered to the perch also needs to be kept an eye on. It is all too easy to tie a leash much too long. There are those, especially beginners, who think it is a kindness to give the hawk as much leash travel as possible. The exact opposite is actually the case. If you allow a hawk sufficient travel to accelerate hard then it can do itself very serious harm. Many Harris Hawks have broken their own legs by bating powerfully and having too long a leash allowing them to be travelling fast enough that the instantaneous stop breaks their bones.

A decent length leash for a Harris Hawk, male or female, will be about five foot long. By the time either one or two falconers knots have been tied the remaining amount of leash will allow plenty of movement without letting the hawk build up a head of steam if it bates.

An adult female Harris Hawk in hot pursuit.

I personally always tie two knots just to be on the safe side. When I was younger one would suffice but now I'm older I always err on the side of caution and tie two. I have to say that in my experience Harris Hawks are second only to Gyr Falcons in being able to undo a falconers knot. As a matter of course I always pull the first knot as tight as I can just in case the hawk gets the second one undone. Some hawks also take to picking at the end of their leashes where the knotted button and leather washer are. But at least this area is very easy to visually check and any fraying resulting from constant picking shows long before the material is in any danger of parting.

There will be occasions when perhaps you may have to shorten the leash length even further such as in the company of other hawks, perhaps at such events as field meets. Hawks that are weathered out together should be kept well apart, that goes without saying. But a hawk that has designs on killing its neighbour can probably reach a great deal further than you think. They need to be far enough apart that even a flailing wing tip can't be grabbed.

Nowadays, most falconers transport their hawks in a travelling box and they really are worth their weight in gold. A hawk in a box is anonymous when you are driving which means you don't get people tail-gating you trying to peer in your car. If you have to stop at a garage for petrol you don't emerge to find a gathering of onlookers surrounding your car and then have to run the gauntlet of the usual inane questions. Travelling more than one hawk can be done in complete safety and it makes you wonder how on earth we got on before we had them. But if you travel your hawk in its box unhooded, then take care when opening the door of the box to take the hawk out. I have seen several hawks fly out over the shoulder of the falconer the instant the box is opened.

If you are on your own when this happens then it should not present too much of a problem. Presumably you have taken your hawk out because you are either going to exercise her or hunt with her. This means she will be keen and should return instantly to the proffered fist but if you are in company with other falconers who are also going to fly their hawks then your hawk could well attack another that is on someone else's fist. I travel my hawks hooded but I also leave their leash and swivel on and attach their leash to the perch inside the box. This way I do not get a nasty shock when I open the door.

When exercising a hawk, particularly in the case of a Harris Hawk which seems to detest all other hawks with a vengeance, make sure they cannot see another tethered hawk or falcon. Be aware of what is around you and what they will be able to see if they go up a tree or onto a nearby building. Also, never forget they are intelligent hawks and most certainly have a very good memory. I knew of someone that had three falcons sitting on his lawn and as he went to go out into the fields behind his house he threw the falcons their daily ration of food. He then passed through a hedge and a small stand of trees into a grass field. He cast the hawk into a tree with the intention of exercising her to the fist. The hawk alighted momentarily in the tree and then flew back to the house and promptly killed one of the falcons on the lawn.

The hawk could not have possibly seen the lawn from the tree; it had gone back because it had seen other hawks with food and knew the area sufficiently to realise where it was in relation to an easy meal. Many times Harris Hawks have proved to me what excellent memories they have. When I was making a video in Scotland some years back we were filming hunting with a very experienced female. The estate held large numbers of Roe deer and some were being culled at the time of the filming. Those shot were gralloched where they went down and consequently we kept coming upon piles of deer guts and innards. The hawk thought that these were wonderful and obviously wanted to go down and see what could be had for free.

Each time we came across some we would quickly bury them, because we were out hawking rabbits we had ferrets with us and a spade so it seemed the most sensible thing to do. One particular pile was right next to a tree with a large hollow in the base. The pile was unceremoniously kicked into the hollow and out of sight and then we walked on and on looking back we could see no evidence of the free meal at all. Not long after we got a decent slip at a rabbit but the hawk fumbled her footing and the rabbit got away. I held up my fist and called for the hawk to return and she immediately took off and headed straight toward me. But instead of returning to the fist she sailed over me and landed at the base of the tree and calmly walked into the hollow. By the time we had run back to her she had consumed sufficient food that flying that day was now out of the question.

I remember on another occasion a friend catching a rabbit with his hawk after we had only been out 10 minutes or so. It was a very warm evening and he didn't want to be carrying a rabbit around with him unnecessarily. So he wedged it in the low fork of a tree and we carried on. Some 200 yards later we kicked up a rabbit out of some long grass and enjoyed a really good flight with the hawk. But the rabbit just made the safety of a hole and left the hawk sitting on the ground peering down into it. On being recalled to the fist this hawk also carried on and went back to the dead rabbit in the tree.

As can be seen from the above, many mistakes in training and out in the field can be avoided with a little thought and attention to detail. As falconers we owe it to our hawks to give them the best possible care and attention. Many of the mistakes we make can lead to an injury or worse to the hawk, which is why it probably pays for a falconer to have a slightly pessimistic outlook on life. If he looks on the blackest side of things and tries to imagine what could possibly go wrong then it will be all that much easier to anticipate any mistakes and therefore avoid them. I have highlighted several bad mistakes here because they have such dire consequences for the hawks involved. But many mistakes we make are just irritating and, like most experiences in life, we can learn from them and make sure they are not repeated. Very occasionally the mistake made will have painful consequences for us as opposed to the hawk.

A momentary distraction or carelessness when feeding a hungry hawk on the fist can have a painful outcome for the falconer doing the feeding. More than once I have seen an ungloved hand grabbed by the hawk as it moves to put more food in this way. As with all things there is a right and a wrong way to present food to a hawk on the fist. If you get it wrong then the hawk may well foot you and the experience will be a far from pleasant one.

I have also seen unprotected hands grabbed when a hawk is on a kill. The first time I saw it happen, luckily to someone else, the falconer was assisting the hawk with taking her reward from a kill. As the hawk was striving to break through the fur of a rabbit she had just caught the falconer nicked the rabbit skin with his knife and then with both hands tore the skin apart. The sudden movement of the hands involved in the tearing motion stimulated the hawk to lash out and grab one of them in its talons. My own hawk was hooded on my fist – she had killed earlier in the day. The gutted rabbit that was in the back of my hawking vest was thrown onto the ground close to the hawk and she left her own rabbit and companion's hand in order to claim her new prize. Luckily, we got the hawk off of the falconer's hand quickly, but it still required a trip to the local hospital for a tetanus injection. The strength of grip of a female Harris Hawk is awesome and has to be felt to be believed.

I witnessed another example of what a lapse of concentration can bring when out hawking with a friend some years back. I was accompanying him and his female Harris Hawk and we were using ferrets in holes along a hedgerow in order to bolt a rabbit for the hawk. The hedgerow was relatively sparse and there were Oak trees dotted along it at intervals of 100 yards or so. The hawk was allowed to take stand in a tree and then a ferret would be introduced to a hole. We had enjoyed one or two flights without any success and the hawk was getting eager and watched every move we made. As we stood back expectantly waiting for a rabbit to bolt we suddenly heard squealing and saw a rabbit half emerge from a hole. My friend realised the ferret had hold of the rabbit by its rear end and went over to sort the situation out. As he grabbed the rabbit the hawk arrived and promptly grabbed him. In the ensuing mêlée, accompanied by much cursing and dire threats, the hawk eventually let go of the falconer and concentrated its attentions on the rabbit. Unfortunately, the ferret wasn't over impressed with the whole affair and decided to bite the falconer for good measure. I have to say the whole episode also caused me some pain – mainly in my side from laughing so much.

chapter twelve
accidents

No matter how careful the falconer is when it comes to looking after the welfare of his hawk sooner or later an accident will occur. Realistically the vast majority of accidents are avoidable with some prior thought being given to certain situations. Nearly all accidents involving hawks are caused by human failings, whether it be a moment's stupidity or just carelessness the result is almost invariably the same, the hawk being the one that will end up suffering the consequences, not the human. Therefore, it certainly does pay to think before you act, or at least it does from the hawks' point of view. I have decided to cover

Adult female Harris Hawk on her kill.

Adult female head study.

a number of accidents that I know have, unfortunately, befallen others in the hope that their unfortunate experiences can be learnt from and therefore be avoided. It is very easy to be wise after an event and accidents are precisely that, accidents.

Three serious accidents I have seen have been the result of throwing food to a hawk whilst it was on its perch. The first two both involve hawks and falcons that were part of display teams that were being fed up at the end of the days performances. Those people that had been giving the displays wandered around the weatherings throwing chicks to the hawks and falcons displayed there. Twice I have seen a Lanner Falcon grabbed by a Harris Hawk who had finished its food and wanted some more. As falcons are slower feeders than hawks the falcon became the centre of the Harris Hawks attention, being tied too closely the Harris was able to reach the Lanner on both occasions.

At the first incident the hawk and the falcon were parted almost immediately and fortunately very little damage was done to the falcon other than giving it a major fright. This happy outcome was more by luck than judgement it has to be said, but the second incident resulted in the loss of the life for the falcon.

Andy King with his female Harris Hawk, Myra.

What compounded the stupidity of the whole event was the display giver trying to pretend to his audience of gathered onlookers that nothing was wrong. Instead of leaping to the aid of the falcon he strolled over and made some inane remark along the lines of "come on now, stop squabbling". I use the term display giver for the very good reason that far from all of those that give falconry displays are actual falconers. Not that it is essential to be a good falconer to be able to give crowd pleasing displays, but I do think that those that hunt with their hawks and falcons have a greater understanding of their needs and also a greater awareness of the things that can go wrong when groups of raptors are in close proximity to each other.

The third incident involving a hawk being thrown food resulted in the hawk breaking its own leg. On this occasion the hawk was one that was being moulted at the bow and instead of being fed on the fist it had been tossed its daily ration of four day old chicks. Two landed within reach of the hawk the other two didn't. The falconer looked out of the window to make sure his hawk was okay some 20 minutes later and noticed the hawk was sitting on the ground with two chicks just out of reach. As he approached the hawk he noticed it was holding one leg up at a strange angle, and the hawk was subsequently taken to a vet where it was eventually discovered that it had broken its leg very high up. The constant frantic bating trying to get at the food had cost the hawk dearly.

The problem was compounded by the fact that the vet the hawk was taken to was not overly experienced when it came to raptors. Having donned a pair of welding gloves he then proceeded to pull the hawk's leg backwards and forwards and then pronounced that the leg was not broken and that an x-ray wasn't necessary. When the falconer asked how that could have been established from a cursory examination he was told that if the leg was broken the hawk would have cried out in pain. Needless to say the hawk was taken to a different vet and an x-ray confirmed that the leg was indeed broken. The break was successfully pinned and after a considerable time the hawk did eventually make a full recovery. A moment's carelessness when throwing food to the hawk had cost the falconer dearly in the pocket and more importantly the hawk had been caused a great deal of needless pain and discomfort.

At least in this case the hawk was able to make a full recovery. Sometimes, the eventual outcome is not always happy and the accident itself is one that is beyond the control of the falconer. A friend of mine was hunting with his male Harris Hawk on a piece of ground he had obtained permission to hunt on. One rabbit was in the bag and as he pressed on with his hawk to try and get another, a pheasant was flushed. The hawk gave chase and in doing so left the wood they were in and flew off across some open ground. When my friend emerged from the wood there was no sight of the hawk. In the distance he could see the backs of some houses and the fences that enclosed the relative rear gardens and on looking at his telemetry receiver it told him that the hawk was somewhere within the cluster of houses. The thoughts that normally flood into the mind of the falconer at a time like this certainly flooded into his. Had his hawk attacked a small pet? Had the hawk been killed by a dog? Had some lout hit it with a stick or shot it with an air weapon? Everything that possibly can go wrong suggests itself at a time like this. As he got to the first rear garden a man appeared and asked him if he was looking for a hawk. If this was the case then he had lured the errant hawk into his garden shed and shut the door. He had been working in his garden when the hawk had landed on the fence and he had realised it was a trained hawk due to the jesses and bells and then had enticed it into the shed. With relief, my friend went to the shed and took his hawk back up onto the fist. He noticed that the hawk had a fair crop and asked the man what he had used to lure the hawk into the shed.

Relieved to hear that it was a small chunk of raw meat my friend set of home with his hawk grateful that a potentially dangerous situation had come to nothing, or so he thought. The next morning the hawk was sitting fluffed up with slitty eyes and repeatedly shivering. A vet was telephoned and due to the symptoms the vet agreed that my friend could bring his hawk in immediately. Despite the fact that it was less than a 20 minute drive to the veterinary surgery the hawk died before my friend could get it there. The post mortem revealed that it was salt poisoning that had killed the hawk and it turned out that the small piece of raw meat had in fact been a chunk of bacon and the salt content had simply proved too much for the hawks system.

The true tragedy of this loss had been the fact that the gardener had been genuinely trying to help and the poisoning was an accident in the true sense of the word. It had never occurred to him that the meat he gave to the hawk would kill it. The man had acted out of kindness and a willingness to help but due to lack of knowledge had ended the life of the hawk.

Another incident that I heard of whilst writing this book also, unfortunately, ended with the hawk in question losing its life. A male Harris Hawk had enjoyed a very successful first season being flown at quarry and had been recently taken up again to embark upon a second. In no time at all the hawk was back in the groove and chasing quarry hard catching a rabbit on its third day back in action. The falconer went to the aid of his hawk and despatched the rabbit by passing a knife through its skull. As the knife was withdrawn the hawk reacted to the movement and footed the knife wrapping one foot around the blade. The knife was very sharp and the resultant cuts led to the hawk bleeding to death very quickly on the spot. A moment

Dale Fairbrass with his adult female Harris Hawk, Anita.

of not being fully aware of what could happen turned out to have terrible consequences for the hawk.

When a hawk is on a kill they are very excited and are quick to react to movement of any kind. Many people do indeed use a knife to despatch any rabbit caught and never have any kind of incident at all. But most of the falconers I know use either a tool such as a screwdriver, which has a point but not a blade, or something similar. Or they rely on the good old fashioned method of stretching the neck of the rabbit. This way there is nothing for the hawk to foot other than the falconers' gloved hand.

The falconer does have a duty to despatch any quarry caught by the hawk as quickly as possible but they also need to balance the safety of the hawk in the method used.

Not all accidents prove to be fatal, at least for the hawk, but can still have dire consequences. I have known of several hawks that have flown into sheep fencing when in hot pursuit of quarry and most have come away with cuts and bruising and very little else to show for their mishaps, but some are not so fortunate and break wings or even necks. Fencing is a major hazard when hawking but to avoid it all together is practically impossible in this day and age. Most hawks have sufficient awareness to avoid it most of the time. But when chasing quarry they are sharply focused, tending to remain unaware of obstacles and this is when most accidents will happen.

I once had a female Harris Hawk sever part of the top mandible when chasing a pheasant through a wood. The pheasant had been accidentally flushed a little way off from us and the hawk gave chase. Several years previously there had been a release pen in the area we were hawking and odd bits and pieces of chicken wire still lay around. In an effort to throw off the attentions of the hawk the pheasant dropped to the ground and ran into a clump of undergrowth. The hawk crashed in after it only to bounce backwards and come to a very sudden stop. Some wire had been left on the ground and vegetation had grown up through it so when the hawk crashed into the wire at full speed it was very fortunate not to have been killed or broken a wing. When I called her back to the fist I noticed her face was covered in blood and that part of her beak was missing.

She was bleeding quite profusely from the wound and only the repeated attentions of a styptic pencil eventually stemmed it. Fortunately, I carry one of these pencils in my hawking vest in the first aid kit I always have with me which I find to be a very useful item and easily and cheaply obtained from any chemists shop. The wound was a nasty one in that the hawk could not eat for herself for a considerable time. The vet I consulted immediately after the incident played with the idea of making an artificial extension to the mandible out of fibre glass and attaching it with a special glue. I wasn't too keen on the sound of this and decided I would rather feed my hawk specially prepared meals by hand until the beak had grown sufficiently for her to able to feed herself again. The meals consisted of the hawk's normal diet but instead of being fed whole it was passed through a fine mincer first. The resulting preparation was more or less the same as you would give to eyass hawks you were raising by hand. This carefully prepared mince was then fed to the hawk on the end of my fingers and this went on for almost three months. The one positive thing to come out of this incident was the special bond that built up between myself and this hawk as a result of the hand feeding, whether it was the great deal of time we spent together or if the hawk was aware that she was totally dependent on me and I was there for her each day I have no way of knowing. But I do know our relationship changed and that this particular hawk trusted me implicitly from then on.

Housing and travelling are two other areas that lend themselves to a careless thought having dire repercussions. A prime example being a friend of mine who lost his exceptionally fine female Harris Hawk to a fox because he made a mistake when ordering the weld mesh wire for the aviary he was constructing. Being an old duffer like me he was brought up on the imperial system of measurement as opposed to the metric version. When he ordered some wire his conversion from imperial to metric was not as it should be and the mesh that was duly delivered was a great deal larger than he had anticipated – instead of being close to one inch square it was slightly over two inches square. Even this larger size was still far too small for any hawk the size of a Harris to be able to get through, and so he used it anyway.

When being turned loose in the aviary the hawk in question would spend a great deal of her time at the front of the aviary. She became very territorial when she was in her aviary and did not like anyone or anything close to the wire but she was absolutely fine when the falconer went into the aviary with a glove on. She would step straight up and allow her jesses leash and swivel to be attached with no problem at all. It was only if you lingered in front of the aviary that she showed signs of not liking the situation. Eventually, it got to the stage that if you stood directly next to the wire she would crash against it in an effort to get you to move.

One morning my friend was awoken by a terrible noise that sounded as if someone was strangling a cat. He rushed out into the garden to discover a fox at the wire of his hawk's aviary. The hawk lay dying on the floor of the aviary and one of its legs lay just outside the wire and the fox ran off with the other leg of the hawk in its mouth. It can only be surmised that the fox had been investigating the chances of getting into the aviary when the hawk had flown at the wire and footed it. The fox had somehow managed to grab the legs of the hawk and literally pulled them off. A sickening and horrible end to an exceedingly fine hawk.

Travelling several hawks together is always a situation that demands the utmost vigilance on the part of the falconer. Thankfully, due to modern travel boxes accidents on journeys are becoming almost a thing of the past, but there are always exceptions of course. Someone I know had a specially designed trailer for travelling several hawks together and this consisted of two rows of boxes, one row on top of the other, totalling about six boxes in all. In front of these was a traditional screen perch which was capable of holding another three hooded falcons if required.

The boxes themselves closed with catches which were getting a little dated, to say the least. Replacing the catches was a job that was always on the verge of getting done but somehow never seemed to. Having been hawking in Scotland the trailer was going to be used to bring back down south not only this persons hawks, but mine as well. We both had Harris Hawks with us for hunting rabbits and also three falcons for hunting grouse and as it turned out, things changed and I had to come back a day early. I had the choice of bringing the hawks with me or leaving them and letting them come down in the comfort of the custom trailer a day later. It would have been easier and more convenient for me to have taken the latter option but I preferred to have the hawks travel with me and accordingly they accompanied me on my journey.

It was one of the best decisions I have ever taken. On the journey south one of the old catches did indeed shake loose and of course it had to be on the box that contained the female Harris Hawk. She had been put into the box without a leash and swivel and consequently once the door was open she was free to go where she wanted. The hooded falcon on the screen perch in front of her had absolutely no chance what so ever of saving its life.

Although travelling boxes, with catches that work, have undoubtedly prevented many accidents it is important that the boxes themselves are properly constructed and used for their intended purpose. I was approached by someone who wanted to buy a travelling box from me and I showed him the box and was told it was very nice but too dear which drew my normal reply that you get what you pay for in life and quality does, unfortunately, cost. Apparently this person's brother-in-law could knock him up something just as good for a fraction of the price.

Unfortunately, the box maker used a very cheap propylene material as the covering for the perch and the box itself was used to keep the hawk in overnight, not just for travelling. The hawk in question was a youngster that was being trained and therefore its weight had been cut down. The box was opened one morning to find the hawk dead inside it. In its hungry state the hawk had picked at the propylene covering on the perch and ingested long strands of it and so the poor hawk had choked to death on the material.

Without doubt one of the most common mistakes of all, especially in the case of the novice falconer, is to take a hawk too low in condition in the belief that the hunger caused will make the hawk hunt better. In fact the exact opposite is true and a hawk that is over hungry does not focus on hunting wild quarry but is just desperate to get a meal from the source it knows best, that is the falconer. I have seen incident after incident where a hawk is just too keen and this is when they can be a danger to those that fly them and others, particularly dogs or ferrets that are employed to help them obtain flights.

I can illustrate this common fault only to well with an anecdote that happened to myself when making a film for a television company several years ago. Someone that owned a small falconry centre had been approached to provide some hawking footage as part of a series on country life, pastimes and pursuits. The centre owner asked myself and a friend if we could help out and come along with a good falcon that would fly pheasant, also a hawk that would take rabbits and pointer if possible. We duly turned up as requested with a Jerkin that was taking pheasants in real style, a female Harris Hawk I had that was particularly good and Emma my reliable old pointer of the English variety.

The morning was to be spent hawking rabbits and it was to be without the use of ferrets. This involved cameramen being positioned on both sides of long hedgerows and then the falconer working towards them. The pointer was going to be used and it was hoped that her coming on point would give the cameramen time to set-up exactly for the shots they wanted. To give the whole process a dummy run it was decided to hawk a small pond which was in amongst some trees and surrounded by rough vegetation that was not too high. This was ideal for the dog to work and the hawk to spot something if there was anything there.

Superb shot of an adult female Harris Hawk in flight.

For some reason, which I have never really understood, the centre owner had brought along a young lad who had in turn brought a young male Harris Hawk with him. The Harris Hawk in question did not look in fine condition and if it were mine then the last thing I would want is for it to appear on television. The hawk's main flight feathers were all broken on the ends and generally speaking the bird was a mess and it also looked very low in condition. It would appear that the lad was going to be given the opportunity to fly his hawk whilst we gave the pond set-up a try. I expressed the opinion that the hawk looked over keen and also enquired as to whether it had ever worked with dogs before. The answer that the hawk had not been fed the day before to ensure that it was keen did not fill me with confidence. As to the question of its behaviour towards dogs I was assured it was fine and there would be no problems. As the dog in question was mine I posed the question twice more and was categorically assured the hawk was fine with dogs and had worked with them before.

The owner of the centre and television director decided between them that the best approach for getting decent filming would be to put the hawk up one of the trees on the edge of the pond and then run the dog underneath it to see if we could get a point. The hawk was duly cast off from the fist and immediately turned and landed back on it again. As it did so it drooped its wings and shook in the classic begging for food behaviour pattern. I suggested that the hawk be given some food to help alleviate its maniacal actions and when asked how much I suggested at least a gutted chick. The hawk was given one chick leg. It took four separate attempts to get it to fly as far as the tree which at this point I suggested we stick to the original plan and use my hawk that was not so ravenously hungry and had also worked with Emma on a daily basis for several years.

It was decided that as the hawk had finally managed to get as far as a tree we would proceed and could I run the dog now. Just for the sake of my own peace of mind I asked one

Adult female Harris Hawk following on.

further time would the hawk be alright with my dog. Quite huffily I was told there would not be a problem so I sent Emma in and within 15 seconds the hawk dropped out of the tree and bound to her face. I got to my dog in seconds and quite literally hurled the hawk away from her. Undeterred, it got back up and bound to her for a second time and again I pulled it off and hurled it away. This time the owner of the hawk reacted and offered a gloved fist with food on it and the hawk flew to him. It goes without saying that the hawk was fed up there and then and put back in its travelling box. The words that passed between myself and the owner of the hawk were colourful to say the least. Fortunately Emma was okay and although her face was awash with blood it was because one of the hawks talons had caught her on the tongue, so it looked far worse than it actually was. The situation could have been horrendous and avoided, the hawk was so hungry it was just simply desperate to eat.

The reader will have noticed that other than a reference to the use of a styptic pencil which I carry as part of my field first aid kit I make no mention of treating a hawk for injuries or minor ailments. There is a very good reason for this, I am not a vet. I don't feel I know enough about veterinary medicine to give out advice on the subject. Also I personally do not believe that chapters on veterinary subjects are suitable material for a falconry book. Vets are very highly trained and if you have any doubts whatsoever about the health or well being of your hawk then you must consult one as soon as possible. Don't forget that all predators are conditioned to hide injuries and weakness from others and therefore by the time the falconer spots his hawk is not 100% fully fit it probably does need professional help.

The leading vets in the field of raptor treatment hold regular day courses with regard to home health and first aid. If the reader has a desire to further his or her knowledge in this direction then I would suggest they attend one of these courses.

chapter thirteen
in the field

Hunting with Harris Hawks has given me so much pleasure over the years that I thought I would draw this book to a close with some anecdotes of flights that have been just that little bit special. Some of the real gems that have become lodged in the brain have been with my own hawks and some have been with other peoples. But it doesn't really matter whose hawk it is or from whose fist the flight started. An exciting flight is still exciting whether you are a participant in some small way or merely a spectator, the pleasure is there to be enjoyed by either.

Adult female Harris Hawk and rabbit.

Immature male Harris Hawk.

A number of years ago I lived in Scotland, having moved there to be able to have access to better hawking ground on a daily basis. I literally used to live on the edge of a grouse moor which started less than three minutes walk behind my cottage. It was here that I used to fly my falcons at grouse, this most difficult of quarry, throughout the relative season. In front of my cottage was 4000 acres of first class hawking ground suitable for flying my female Harris. During the grouse hawking season I would hunt with my Harris Hawk every morning before going out on the hill with the falcons in the afternoon. For the rest of the hawking season I would hunt my Harris every day except Sundays. This rest day was not because I'm religious but the local people tended to be there and there seemed no point in upsetting them merely to get another days hawking each week. Also, I firmly believe it does the hawk and the dogs good to have a day off once a week.

The result of this intense quality hawking was that my hawk was super fit and I suddenly found I had a lot of falconer friends who wanted to come and stay for the week and bring their hawk. One particular pairing that came to stay was a falconer I didn't know too well along with

Adult female Harris Hawk on rabbit.

his intermewed female Goshawk and his apprentice falconer who was flying a young female Harris Hawk. The apprentice I had never met before but it didn't take too long to appreciate that he was extremely serious about his falconry and absorbed information like a sponge. His Harris Hawk was certainly fit and caught rabbits well and he expressed a wish to try and catch either a blue or a brown hare with his hawk and was ridiculed by his mentor. Instead of being encouraged to try with the blue but warned of likelihood of his hawk not wishing to tackle the brown, his mentor obviously thought it better to laugh at him in front of others. The falconer with the Goshawk was visiting some other falconers on a nearby estate the next day and would not be back until after dark. I told the lad I would take my old pointer out with him in the morning and we would see if we could get him a close slip at a blue hare.

Next day, before going off with his Goshawk, the falconer had two or three more sarcastic little niggles at his apprentice about trying to catch hares with his Harris Hawk. I ran my pointer on the edge of the moor where I would frequently find both blue and the occasional brown hare. My dog soon came on point and the slight wagging of her tail told me it was ground game she was pointing.

Myself and the lad moved so that we approached the dog from an uphill position in order to try and encourage whatever was being pointed to run down hill. We managed to get in really close before a blue hare shot out of its seat and endeavoured to get away from us, but the Harris Hawk was off like lightening and had bound to it before it had gone 30 feet. The lad was on hand in seconds to despatch the hare and see to his hawk. The hawk had subdued the hare well enough for the short while it was unassisted and the lad really wanted to try for another one. I expressed an opinion that as it was the first ever hare the hawk had taken

An adult male Harris Hawk after an unsuccessful attempt to hold onto a Mallard drake that took him into a stream.

perhaps she should be allowed to take her pleasure on it as a reward. But the lad felt it would be poetic justice if he managed to catch not just one but two hares to show his supposed tutor. He asked if we could just try and fly one more point and he would stop, then feed his hawk up regardless of the outcome.

I encouraged my dog to run on and find game again and it didn't take too long to get another point. The tail was wagging gently so it was definitely fur in front of her and another careful approach was made, only this time the hare broke before we could get up close, it was a brown hare and it galloped off very quickly. The hawk instantaneously gave chase and caught up with the hare in no time then the hare jinked and managed to throw the extremely determined hawk off twice before she bound to it. When she did finally bind to the hare she was quite a way off from us. The lad sprinted for all he was worth afraid that his hawk would get kicked off before he could get there and give her some help. The hawk was not in the mood to let go, no matter how hard the hare struggled, and hung on until help arrived. This time the hawk was allowed to take a full crop on her kill and it was one very happy young falconer that made his way back to the cottage that morning. This young lad has since gone on to become a fine and extremely dedicated falconer and a credit to the sport.

Taking on apprentices can be a very rewarding process and helping guide a novice falconer into a competent one is very satisfying. My last apprentice appeared out of the blue several years ago and quite literally turned up on my doorstep. He introduced himself and asked if it would be possible for me to help him become a falconer. This is a question I get asked two or three times each year and my initial answer is always the same. Go away and think about it seriously and if you are still keen come back in six months. This person did come back and he started coming hawking with me on a regular basis. At the end of a full season with me he expressed an interest in getting his own hawk and started building an aviary and a weathering as well as making a start on getting all the required falconry furniture together. Each week he would buy something towards his hawking future and as well as this he started going round local farms trying to get permission to hunt when he did eventually get a hawk of his own.

When the time was right for my apprentice to get his first hawk I contacted a friend and managed to get him a female for next to nothing. I felt that he had worked so hard towards the arrival of the hawk that a little help wouldn't go amiss. For the last three hawking seasons I have had the pleasure of watching this hawking combination become better and better at working together and it is rewarding to pass your own knowledge on and watch it be put into practice. The apprentice in question is Andy King and the hawk is Myra.

Myra has become a very good hunting hawk because she is flown so regularly and in all conditions and she is about as far removed from a fair weather hawk as it is possible to be. I have been fortunate enough to see her make several kills that are so outstanding that they lodge in the mind and she is also the only hawk I have ever seen drown a rabbit and not just once, but indeed, twice. Both times it was whilst hawking in Caithness but the incidents were a year apart.

The first was on a clear bright November day when our hawking group consisted of Andy with Myra, myself with Maud and also three other falconers without hawks. Also, joining us was a local artist who wanted to get some photos as references for a hawking scene he had in

Caithness, good rabbit country.

mind to paint. We were hawking some grassy hillocks that led down to a shallow but very fast running burn that was just that little bit too wide to be able to jump across.

Ferrets had been put down a likely looking hole and we stood back in anticipation then a rabbit bolted from a hole that was some way behind us and down the slope. Myra reacted quickly and was off in pursuit. As the hawk closed the gap both the rabbit and her disappeared over the brow of a hillock and were lost to sight. We ran to a spot were they had cleared the brow and looked down upon a bank that ran quite steeply to the burn – neither rabbit nor hawk was in sight.

Once over the brow we were faced with completely open ground to our left and a miniature valley to our right which bent away from us. Everyone assumed that the rabbit had led the hawk around the corner and gave chase. Andy and myself decided to get the telemetry receiver out and have a quick check before dashing off and sure enough we got a pulsing signal standing where we were without even having to extend the aerial. The hawk was very close, literally within a few feet. Right at our feet was a large hole with fresh rabbit droppings all around and for a few moments we feared the worst. Quite a number of Harris Hawks and Red tails have died because they followed their quarry down a hole, having got a certain way in they are unable to turn round and keep on going. Sometimes it is possible to dig them out but all too many have died in this situation.

Andy started to call at the mouth of the hole as I continued with the set trying to get an accurate location and I just happened to look in the burn and saw there the reflection of a hawk's head. Leaning over the bank I was greeted by the sight of Myra quite literally up to the shoulders of her wings in the water. Andy thrust both hands into the water to lift her out only to discover she had the rabbit firmly in her grasp. The rabbit was completely lifeless and the hawk had obviously held it under the water until it had stopped struggling.

Just over a year later on the same estate another rabbit was despatched in more or less the same way. This rabbit had been bolted from some Marram grass and had jumped a small ditch and then scrambled up onto a dry stone wall. The hawk had tried to grab it there but the rabbit leapt from the wall and ran to a ditch with the hawk following closely. The rabbit appeared to have made good its escape when it went into a patch of gorse bushes that lined the bottom and one side of the ditch. The hawk crashed in after the rabbit and for a split second we heard the tell tale scream that normally signifies that the hawk has been successful. But the scream was only momentary and we all assumed that the hawk had fumbled its footing. After several minutes the hawk did not re-appear and we could not hear any movement of bells. Peering into the gorse bushes did no good as they were too thick and so it was out with the telemetry. The signal guided us to a patch of gorse that had spread across the bottom of the ditch that was filled to the height of about 10 inches with water. But we still couldn't see the hawk. Careful cutting away of smaller branches eventually revealed Myra standing in the water clutching her drowned rabbit.

Many Harris Hawks are reluctant to fly quarry hard when there is a decent covering of snow on the ground. They are unwilling to actually come down in it and will often over fly quarry and let simple kills get away. Myra was like this the first time she hunted in thick snow and let three rabbits go one after the other. So she had to have a little confidence training to help her on her way to decent hawking again and this was simple enough to arrange. Andy and myself cleared a patch of snow from a road so that there was only a thin covering on top of it, then we got a freshly killed rabbit, gutted it and opened it up. We fashioned a hollowed out mound on the side of the road and installed our deceased rabbit in it. Attached to the rabbit was a creance line and I went off some 20 yards or so with the other end of the creance. Andy approached with Mrya on the fist and I suddenly pulled the rabbit into view and up the road. Myra gave chase instantly closed on the rabbit but landed beside it before jumping into it.

She was allowed to have a few mouthfuls from the rabbit and was then taken back up on the fist. Whilst Andy walked off some distance the rabbit was repositioned in his make shift home and then when Myra was walked back again the rabbit popped out of his home and made his way back up the road again. This time the hawk was after it in earnest and grabbed the carcase with both feet. Again she was allowed a few mouthfuls and then taken off once again. On the third run I dragged the rabbit across a patch of snow that hadn't been cleared and the hawk took the rabbit as she normally would. She was allowed to take the rest of her meal on it and we would try hunting for real again the next day.

The following morning we managed to ferret four rabbits and Myra took three of them in style. The little exercise from the day before had given her the confidence required to come down in the snow and she has never worried about it since. As is so often the case, a little care and attention can quite easily overcome what can seem a major problem. The thing to do is try and look at the predicament from the point of view of the hawk and then address it accordingly.

Over the many enjoyable years of flying my old faithful female Harris Hawk Maud I have had the pleasure of innumerable special moments and flights. The most difficult problem I have had is to pick just a few from the many to relate here.

One of which occurred when I was involved with some rabbit clearance work on a high security restricted site. Due to the nature of the premises it was only possible to remove the rabbits with either ferrets or hawks, or a combination thereof. A rabbit had been flushed from underneath some large diameter pipes and ran across a roadway heading for a jungle of yet more metal pipes and stairways. Maud gave chase the moment she saw the rabbit and closed on it rapidly. The rabbit was aware the hawk was getting dangerously close and ducked beneath an Armco metal barrier in an attempt to throw her off. Maud folded her wings and appeared to scrape under the Armco as well, but only just. The rabbit then pulled off a move which should have ensured its safety, it literally ran beneath the bottom step of a metal stairway. The hawk closed on the stairway and I realised she wasn't going to stop. She closed her wings and somehow managed to squeeze between the small gap between two steps. I really couldn't believe it was possible for the hawk to get through such a small space and survive and I ran over with a feeling of dread which was enhanced by the fact that there was no tell tale squeal to tell me the hawk had caught her prey. I envisaged Maud with broken bones at the very least.

But I need not have worried; Maud was sitting on her prey completely unscathed, but just how she managed to negotiate two such tight obstacles and still catch her prey without breaking so much as feather is beyond me. Hawks can get through narrow gaps with amazing dexterity. My male Harris Hawk, Dodgy, once chased a cock pheasant which flew over a wall and then appeared briefly the other side of a traditional five bar gate. He flew directly towards the gate and closed his wings and passed between two bars of the gate – something I would not have thought possible had I not have seen it for myself.

Along with many other Harris Hawks Maud has the incredibly irritating habit of flattening herself on a kill if the quarry is taken some distance away from me and then keeping as still as possible as I approach. This particular trait almost certainly saved her life on one occasion. A friend of mine asked if he could borrow Maud for a while as his own hawk had suffered a broken leg and would obviously be out of action for some considerable time. I was due to go off to do some hawking in Mexico and agreed he could borrow my hawk for a month or so.

My friend was out hawking with Maud when she chased a pheasant into a large wood and, having failed to catch it, flew on out the other side and ended up on the edge of a smallholding. When my friend arrived on the scene he knew that he was close to Maud because he had briefly heard the bells as he ran over. Unfortunately, he had left the telemetry receiver in his car and was trying to locate the hawk in the traditional manner. Search as hard as he could he could not find Maud although he knew he must be extremely close. In the meantime the owner of the smallholding came over to ask what he was doing and having explained the predicament my friend was amazed to see the transformation that overtook the smallholder. Apparently he hated hawks with a passion and certainly was not going to tolerate one on his land. He had supposedly lost a great many of his Guinea Fowl and Peacock chicks to wild hawks, presumably Sparrowhawks, and therefore detested hawks of all kinds. Despite my friend explaining the legal situation of deliberately harming a hawk, trained or otherwise, the smallholder was not to be placated. If he saw the hawk first on his land then he felt it was his right to shoot it. As the discussion heated up my friend caught a slight movement out of the corner of his eye. Maud was laying flat on an adult Guinea Fowl that she had obviously killed. Fortunately, she was in the bottom of a small ditch and almost impossible to spot if she did not move. If the smallholder were to see Maud then a particularly nasty situation could well have developed.

My friend kept his head and also tried to keep the small holder engaged in conversation so after several minutes the opinion was expressed that the hawk must have moved on and therefore he was better of looking for her elsewhere and with nerves of steel he turned his back on the situation and walked away. Looking back, he saw that the belligerent smallholder was heading back to his cottage so he quickly sprinted over to Maud, scooped her up without ceremony, and got out of the area as quickly as possible. Had Maud not chosen this occasion as one of those where she prefers to hide her presence then this anecdote may well have had a much more depressing outcome. Also, of course, it has to be said that had my friend carried the telemetry receiver with him instead of leaving it in the car then the situation would never have arisen.

The two kills that I remember above the many others Maud has made are as different as they are memorable. The first was when I was making a video with a film company on Harris Hawking. The director, a non falconer, had very clear ideas as to what he wanted and what made good copy and these tended to differ from mine quite considerably, particularly as to what footage was to be included in the final product and what was to be binned. Having filmed all the boring sections like housing and equipment the following six days were to be spent purely and simply filming hunting with various Harris Hawks. Males and females on their own, also a cast of hawks and finally a group of hawks. As I don't like group hawking I gave this section a miss but agreed to take part in the solitary hawking sections and also agreed to fly Maud in a cast with the male hawk of a friend of mine.

The days filming had been going quite well and both Maud and the male had caught a rabbit a piece. We had moved on to a large area of rough grass that was interspersed with small clumps of Gorse bushes and Marram grass. Before myself and the friend set out to hunt the area we had to wait whilst the two cameramen took up their positions. Once they were in place we walked forward with the hawks. Almost immediately a rabbit broke close to me and Maud was off in hot pursuit. The rabbit just managed to make the safety of a very small gorse bush and ran out the other side as the hawk crashed into it. The male Harris Hawk spotted the rabbit trying to make its escape and was after it immediately and in the meantime Maud ran round the gorse bush looking for her quarry. When she couldn't find it she took to the air and pumped upwards to around 30 feet. From this slightly elevated height she soon spotted the rabbit again and made off after it but unfortunately, by now she was some 200 yards or so behind it.

The male had caught up with the rabbit and made his move. At precisely the right moment the rabbit jinked and the male was unceremoniously dumped on the ground. Maud was flying as hard as she could and closed on the rabbit rapidly and she passed the grounded male and took the rabbit just before it reached a huge gorse hedge. When hawk and rabbit came to a standstill they were literally inches from the gorse, another couple of seconds and the rabbit would have been safe. I paced out the total length of the flight afterwards and it was some 420 yards.

The other kill that particularly stands out in my mind took place in the very north of Scotland in the depths of winter. I was hawking with a group of friends and we had been enjoying some excellent sport as well as companionship. Our party consisted of several Harris Hawks, a couple of Goshawks and a male Black Eagle. Helping to provide flights were a pointer, a Brittany and several ferrets. We were hawking the side of a large and exceedingly steep grassy bank beside a large loch. Several rabbits had been ferreted and flown but all had managed to evade the best attentions of the hawks and eagle. Maud was next up to fly and I stood on top of the grass bank waiting for a rabbit to bolt after a ferret had been put down a likely looking hole.

A rabbit was eventually bolted and it made straight down the slope towards a ridge above the side of the loch. Over the ridge was a drop of 20 feet or so down to a narrow grass strip that ran along the edge of the water. Despite the proximity of the water there were several holes that were obviously in use by rabbits. Maud really flew hard and took the rabbit just as it reached the ridge and then the momentum of the actual strike took both her and the rabbit over the edge into fresh air where both of them seemed to hang in space a second before they started to plummet downwards. 'Maud' released her grip on the rabbit just before they both hit the ground and grabbed hold of it again the instant it had done so.

These are just some of the kills that stand out in my memory from a great number I have enjoyed over the years. There are an equal number of flights that also stand out that did not result in the hawk killing the intended quarry. Hawking is enjoyable because of the infinite variety of the flights that can be enjoyed, so when you are out in the field you never know what the next flight might produce and that is all part of the enjoyment.

A successful conclusion.

chapter fourteen
tailpiece

H awking is a sport in which we never ever stop learning and it always has something to teach us. The more a falconer actually practises his sport the more he will be able to learn and he should ensure his mind is always open to absorbing knowledge. This book is the distillation of knowledge gained from nearly 40 years as a practising falconer and was written in the hope that it may be of interest to those that share a passion for the sport that I hold dear. I make no apologies for any shortcomings, the book may have as any written work must, by its very nature, be a very personal view.

An apology that I must make is, when speaking generally, for constantly referring to falconers as masculine and the hawks themselves as feminine. This is not out of chauvinism but in the interest of brevity and lack of continuous boring repetition. Gender makes no difference what so ever as to whether someone will make a good falconer or not. It has far more to do with a determination to succeed and an empathy with hawks themselves that really matters.

The important thing for any would be falconer is a desire to carry out the sport of falconry to the very best of their ability and to always have the interest of their hawk upper most in their mind. The sport itself is without doubt one of the oldest, second only to coursing I should imagine. Every falconer owes it to those that have practised the sport before him and those that are yet to do so, not to bring the sport into disrepute. This ancient pastime does not lend itself to those that would dabble with it and such an approach will never bring results to be proud of. Most falconers that I am fortunate enough know are proud of what they do and are protective towards their sport. They also want to ensure that the skills learnt over the years are passed on to future generations. To this end I would urge my fellow falconers to help the genuine would-be enthusiast along their way. It doesn't take a great deal of probing to separate the temporarily fired up enquirer from the potential falconer. I can speak from experience when I say it really does give a great deal of satisfaction to take on a complete beginner and watch them gradually grow into an accomplished falconer.

I realise that it is a far from popular view but I believe there should be some form of restriction on the way in which hawks can be obtained. Most countries that recognise the sport of falconry as a meaningful pastime, have either some form of apprenticeship for those who wish to become falconers, or legislation relating to how hawks can be obtained and owned. It would appear that in Britain many people see any such move towards this type of legislation as restricting the freedom of the individual. I think that any laws that help ensure the future welfare of both the sport of falconry and the hawks themselves is a good thing. If people are

A superb female Harris Hawk.

confident in their own abilities or intentions and how they house and look after their hawks what on earth do they have to fear? There are plenty of laws relating to shooting and fishing and neither of these sports seems to have suffered as a result of them. In the case of fishing, licence fees have contributed greatly to the improvement of sporting facilities and the quality of fishing available. Legislation doesn't have to be draconian to improve and safeguard our sport. Like many others I do truly fear that if falconers are not seen to put their own house in order then sooner or later a government department will do it for them. We may well then be faced with laws that are unsuitable and extremely restricting.

With domestic production of hawks now a matter of course there are a great many new hawks coming onto the market each year. Consequently prices have dropped dramatically and now put certain species of hawk well within the range of those that think perhaps they might give hawking a go. In many cases Harris Hawks are cheaper than lurcher puppies and when prices were far higher only someone who really wanted a Harris Hawk got one because of the serious outlay required. I personally have purchased male Harris Hawks for £50.00 and females for £75.00. At these sorts of prices no wonder a great many hawks get dabbled with and then get passed from pillar to post.

I have known of far too many hawks that have been bought on a whim and then passed on as soon as things become too much for their owners. In the last 12 months I have had seven Harris Hawks temporarily reside with me whilst I find them new and more appreciative homes. One of these was quite literally dumped on me when the owner turned up at my door one evening and stated that either I take it or he would cut its anklets off and let it go. The poor hawk in question had been bought for £50.00 from someone else who had passed it on after a brief ownership. It eventually transpired that I was the fourth owner of the hawk which was still in its exceedingly battered juvenile plumage. Luckily, I managed to find a suitable owner who cares for him and has given him stability as well as a decent imping session. The hawk, now known as Rewind due to starting out on life again, is involved in display work at weekends and goes hunting most days of the week.

There are several people that I would like to thank who have contributed either directly or indirectly to the inception and completion of this book. Andy King and Dale Fairbrass here in Great Britain. Martin Guzman, Juan Berumen and Rodrigo Munro Wilson in Mexico. Oscar Beingola in Peru and Quilherme Qeuiroz in Brazil. A very special thanks must go to my friend and fellow falconer Diana Durman-Walters who painstakingly proof read the book and offered help and encouragement when required.

I stated in the introduction to this book that I always welcome genuine constructive criticism and am always interested to hear new ideas or anecdotes from other falconers.

To this end, any reader who wishes to do so can contact me at:

bobdalton@falconleisure.fsnet.co.uk

I sincerely hope that readers have enjoyed the book and have found it of use.